FACTiViTY
ATLAS
EXPLORE
THE WONDERS
OF YOUR
WORLD

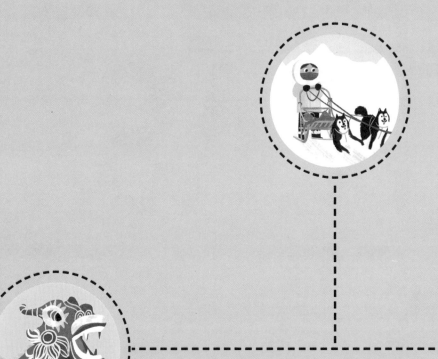

This edition published by Parragon Books Ltd in 2016 and distributed by

Parragon Inc.
440 Park Avenue South, 13th Floor
New York, NY 10016
www.parragon.com

Written by Anita Ganeri
Illustrated by Genie Espinosa
Edited by Claire Hawcock and Michael Diggle
Designed by Duck Egg Blue and Simon Oliver
Production by Jonathan Wakeham
Consultant cartographer: Jenny Slater

ISBN 978-1-4748-2039-4

Printed in China

Discovery KIDS™

 **FACTIVITY™**

ATLAS
EXPLORE
THE WONDERS
OF YOUR
WORLD

PaRragon

Bath · New York · Cologne · Melbourne · Delhi
Hong Kong · Shenzhen · Singapore

Contents

The pages in **bold** show you amazing maps of the world!

You'll find answers to the activities at the back of the book.

Learn more about some famous landmarks on page 124.

Travel the world

Are you ready for an adventure? Journey to the four corners of the world in this trip of a lifetime and discover its incredible wonders. Here are all the amazing things you're going to do!

Go tracking

Drive a dogsled

Build an igloo

NORTH AMERICA

Eye up the skyline

Ride the Métro

Paint a cave

Hop on a gondo

Visit the Falls

Take a taxi

PACIFIC OCEAN

Discover dinosaurs

Trek the Sahara

AFRICA

Dive underground

Spot a hurricane

ATLANTIC OCEAN

Navigate a canal

The land on planet Earth is split up into seven huge chunks called continents.

Canoe the Amazon

Trek the Andes

SOUTH AMERICA

Meet a gaucho

SOUTHERN OCEAN

0   500   1,000
miles

Watch the penguins

Be a scientist

Mapping it

A map is a diagram of a part of the world, seen from above. It often shows important places and features you will find there, such as mountains, rivers, roads, or train stations. Using a map helps you find your way around!

The world is developing all the time, so maps need updating regularly to keep the information accurate.

TYPES OF MAP

Because the world is shaped like a ball, a globe is a good way of showing it.

Physical maps show mountains, rivers, lakes, and the height of the land.

This map shows a simplified plan of subway lines and stations. It's called a topological map.

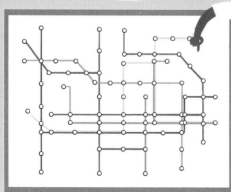

This road map shows where all the roads, airports, and places of interest are.

Here's what the maps in this book look like. The patches of color show you different types of environment, such as deserts and mountains.

The globe and compass give you a quick view of where on the planet you are and which way is north, south, east, and west.

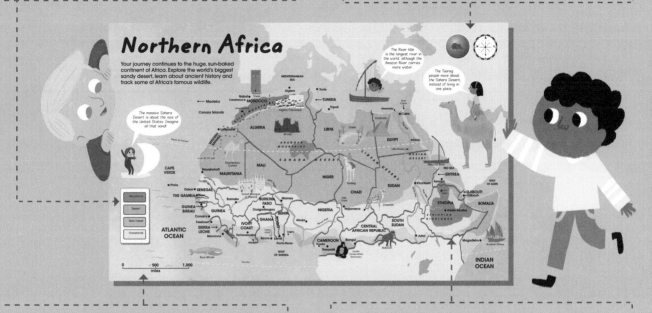

Northern Africa

Your journey continues to the huge, sun-baked continent of Africa. Explore the world's biggest sandy desert, learn about ancient history and track some of Africa's famous wildlife.

This line is called a scale. It helps you work out how large the area you are looking at really is.

There are more than 190 countries in the world. The maps in this book show their boundaries in red.

FLAGS OF THE WORLD

Design a flag for a new country.

Every country has its own flag, with the color and design having special meaning. For example, the 50 stars on the United States of America's flag stand for its 50 states.

Australia

Russian Federation

United Kingdom

United States of America

Brazil

China

India

Germany

Cross the oceans

To travel around the world you have to cross a lot of water. Two-thirds of the world is covered in the stuff. Most of the world's water is in the oceans and to travel across them, you have to fly on a plane or sail by boat.

Don't forget to pack your passport. Everyone needs a record of who they are when they travel around the world.

PACIFIC OCEAN

Gray whale

The Pacific Ocean is the largest body of water in the world, covering one-third of Earth. It's also the deepest. Jellyfish, sharks, rays, and the gray whale live here.

ATLANTIC OCEAN

Atlantic white shark

The Atlantic Ocean has an underwater mountain range, called the Mid–Atlantic Ridge, running down its length. It's home to many large fish including the Atlantic white shark.

SOUTHERN OCEAN

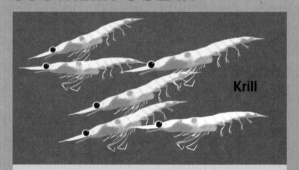

Krill

The Southern Ocean wraps around Antarctica. During winter, half of the ocean is covered in icebergs and ice. Penguins swim here and whales come to feed on krill.

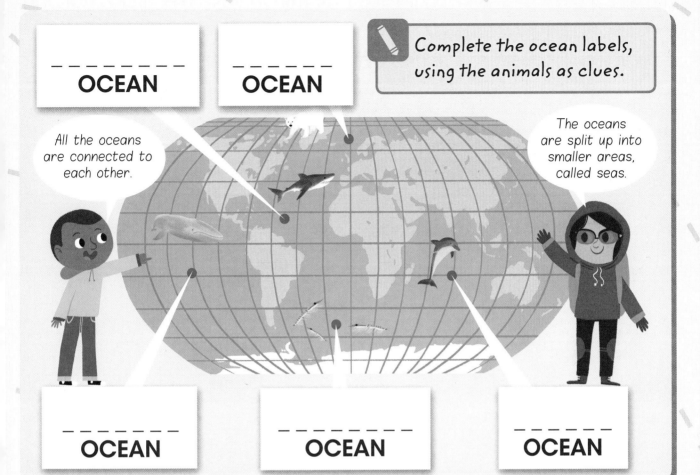

_ _ _ _ _ _ _ _ **OCEAN**

_ _ _ _ _ _ **OCEAN**

Complete the ocean labels, using the animals as clues.

All the oceans are connected to each other.

The oceans are split up into smaller areas, called seas.

_ _ _ _ _ _ _ _ **OCEAN**

_ _ _ _ _ _ _ _ **OCEAN**

_ _ _ _ _ _ **OCEAN**

ARCTIC OCEAN

Polar bear

The Arctic Ocean is the smallest and shallowest ocean. It reaches across the Arctic Circle and is covered in ice most of the year. Seals, polar bears, walruses, and whales live here.

INDIAN OCEAN

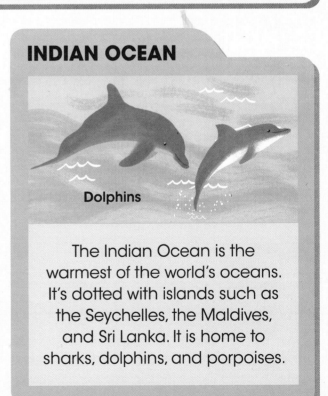

Dolphins

The Indian Ocean is the warmest of the world's oceans. It's dotted with islands such as the Seychelles, the Maldives, and Sri Lanka. It is home to sharks, dolphins, and porpoises.

North America

Welcome to North America, home to two enormous countries—Canada and the United States. You'll find epic natural wonders, from the Grand Canyon to Niagara Falls, and dazzling cities like New York, with its iconic Statue of Liberty landmark.

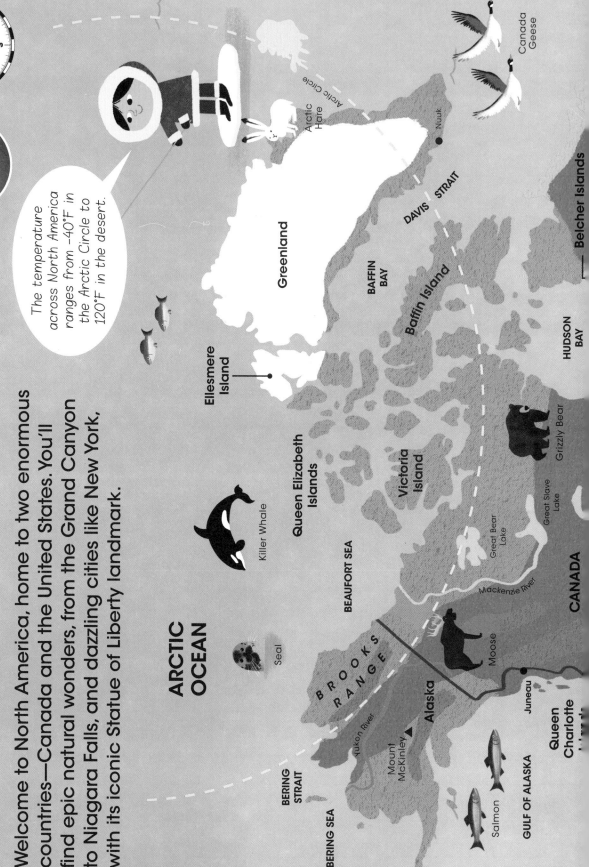

The temperature across North America ranges from –40°F in the Arctic Circle to 120°F in the desert.

Canada Geese

Arctic Circle

Nuuk

Greenland

Arctic Hare

BAFFIN BAY

Baffin Island

DAVIS STRAIT

Belcher Islands

HUDSON BAY

Ellesmere Island

Queen Elizabeth Islands

Victoria Island

Great Bear Lake

Great Slave Lake

Grizzly Bear

Killer Whale

BEAUFORT SEA

Mackenzie River

CANADA

ARCTIC OCEAN

Seal

BROOKS RANGE

Moose

Alaska

Yukon River

Mount McKinley

Juneau

BERING STRAIT

BERING SEA

GULF OF ALASKA

Queen Charlotte

Salmon

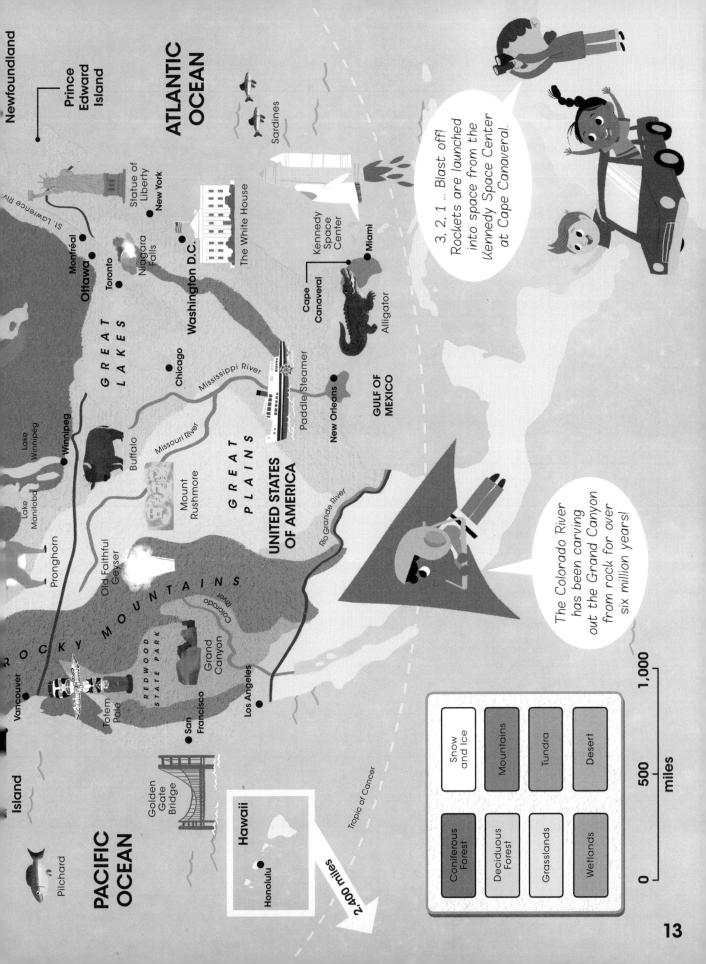

Take a taxi

Your first stop is Manhattan Island, at the heart of New York City. It's packed with skyscrapers, people, and exciting things to explore. The best way to see the sights is in a yellow cab. Taxi!

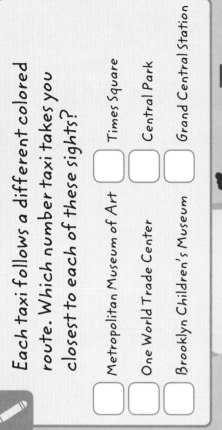

Each taxi follows a different colored route. Which number taxi takes you closest to each of these sights?

	Times Square
	Central Park
	Grand Central Station

	Metropolitan Museum of Art
	One World Trade Center
	Brooklyn Children's Museum

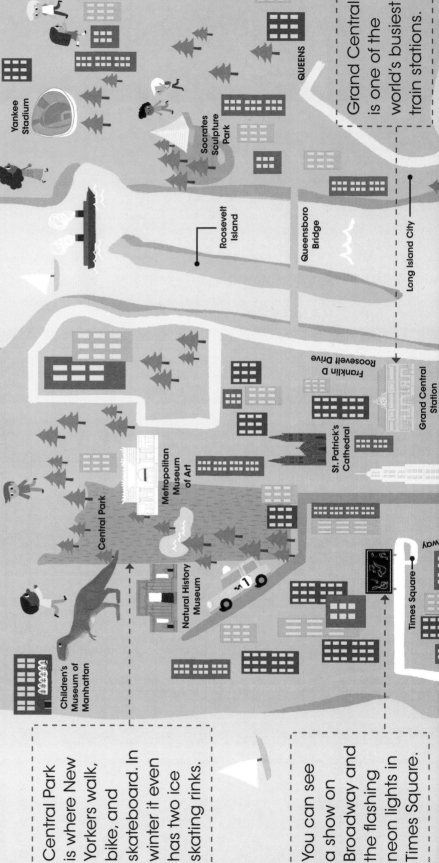

Central Park is where New Yorkers walk, bike, and skateboard. In winter it even has two ice skating rinks.

You can see a show on Broadway and the flashing neon lights in Times Square.

Grand Central is one of the world's busiest train stations.

Children's Museum of Manhattan

Central Park

Natural History Museum

Metropolitan Museum of Art

St. Patrick's Cathedral

Grand Central Station

Franklin D Roosevelt Drive

Times Square

Yankee Stadium

Socrates Sculpture Park

QUEENS

Roosevelt Island

Queensboro Bridge

Long Island City

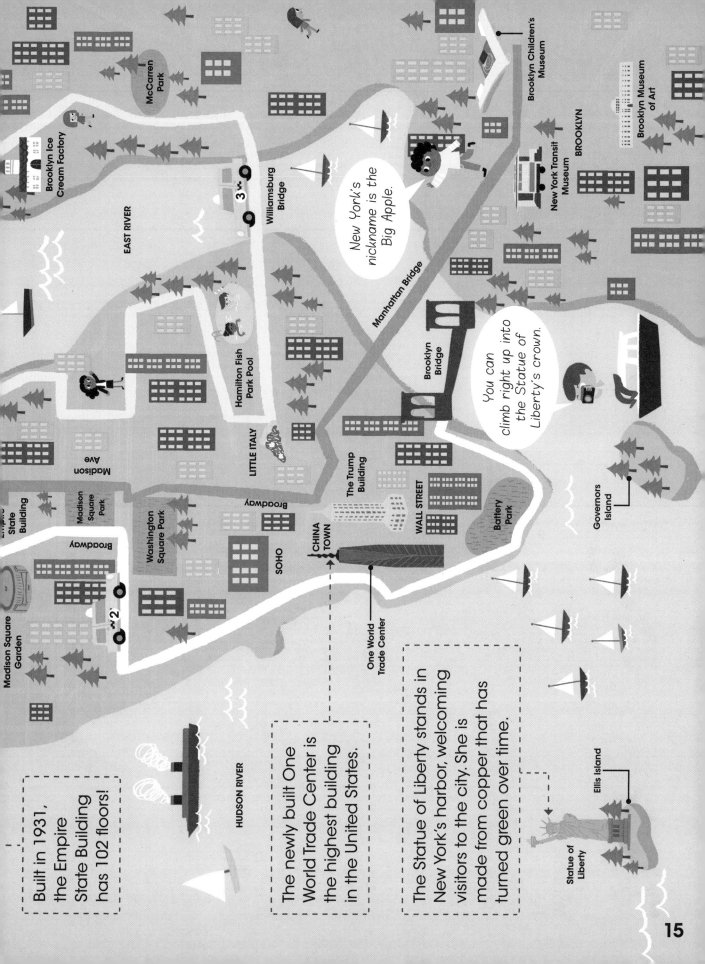

15

Visit the Falls

The spectacular Niagara Falls is actually made up of three separate waterfalls—Horseshoe Falls, American Falls, and Bridal Veil Falls. Water plunges from a height greater than the Statue of Liberty.

An enormous amount of water flows over the Falls—enough to fill 650 Olympic-sized swimming pools every minute!

You can view the Falls from an observation platform, and get even closer on special helicopter and boat tours.

Don't forget your raincoat—you might get soaking wet!

Rainbows are often seen when sunlight catches the spray of water from the Falls.

As the water flows over the Falls, its energy is turned into electricity at a power station.

The energy produced by the power station could run 24 million light bulbs non-stop.

Make your own rainbow.

You will need:
- A glass of water
- Plain paper
- Sunlight

1 Find a window with sunlight shining through it.

2 Move the glass of water above the paper until the sunlight passes through the glass and forms a rainbow of colors on the paper.

3 Try holding the glass of water at different heights and angles to see if it changes the rainbow. Be careful not to spill the water!

Discover dinosaurs

Millions of years ago, North America was home to dinosaurs and other prehistoric creatures. Today, scientists share their exciting dinosaur discoveries in museums such as Chicago's Field Museum.

When a dinosaur died, the soft parts of its body rotted away. Over time, the hard parts, such as bones, were covered in sand and mud and eventually turned into fossils.

TYRANNOSAURUS REX

Uncover the hidden dinosaur by coloring in the shapes containing dots.

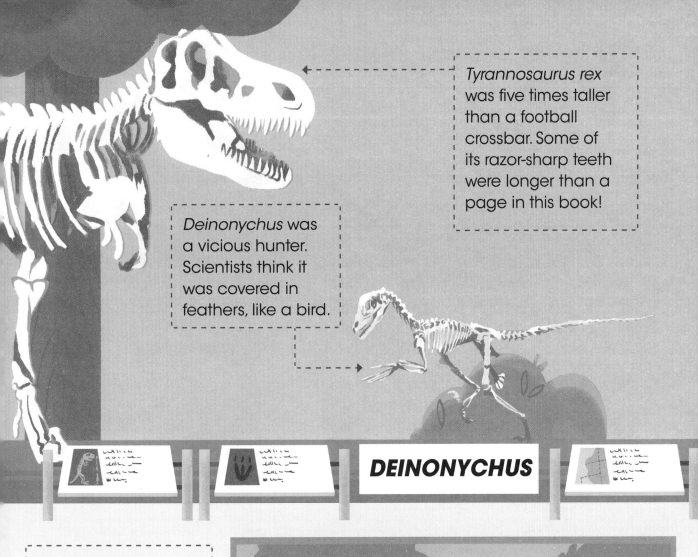

Tyrannosaurus rex was five times taller than a football crossbar. Some of its razor-sharp teeth were longer than a page in this book!

Deinonychus was a vicious hunter. Scientists think it was covered in feathers, like a bird.

DEINONYCHUS

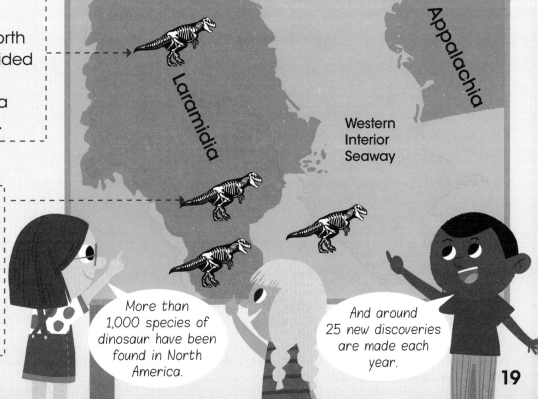

When dinosaurs lived on Earth, North America was divided by sea into two islands: Laramidia and Appalachia.

Appalachia

Laramidia

Western Interior Seaway

When scientists uncover dinosaur fossils, they plot their find on maps to show where the dinosaurs lived.

More than 1,000 species of dinosaur have been found in North America.

And around 25 new discoveries are made each year.

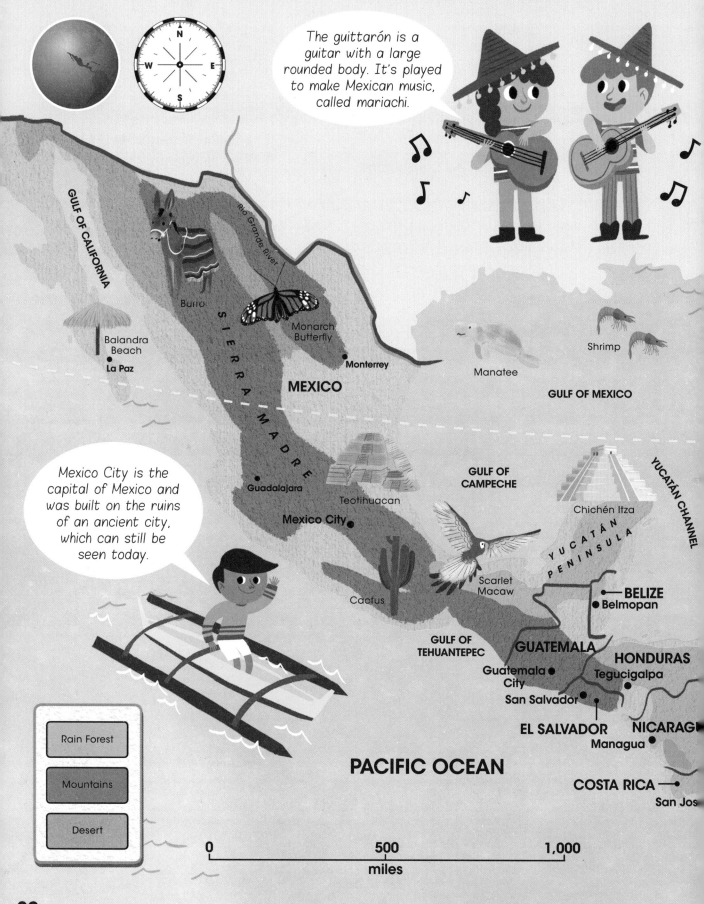

The guittarón is a guitar with a large rounded body. It's played to make Mexican music, called mariachi.

Mexico City is the capital of Mexico and was built on the ruins of an ancient city, which can still be seen today.

GULF OF CALIFORNIA

Rio Grande River

Burro

Monarch Butterfly

SIERRA MADRE

Balandra Beach

La Paz

Monterrey

MEXICO

Manatee

Shrimp

GULF OF MEXICO

GULF OF CAMPECHE

Guadalajara

Teotihuacan

Mexico City

Chichén Itza

YUCATÁN PENINSULA

YUCATÁN CHANNEL

Scarlet Macaw

Cactus

BELIZE

Belmopan

GULF OF TEHUANTEPEC

GUATEMALA

HONDURAS

Guatemala City

Tegucigalpa

San Salvador

EL SALVADOR

NICARAG

Managua

PACIFIC OCEAN

COSTA RICA

San Jos

Rain Forest

Mountains

Desert

0   500   1,000

miles

Mexico and Central America

There is so much to explore in the long stretch of land that links North America to South America—from jungles, deserts, and ancient ruins to crowded cities holding vibrant festivals. To the east is a string of more than 700 beautiful islands called the Caribbean.

ATLANTIC OCEAN

Tropic of Cancer

STRAITS OF FLORIDA

Nassau

THE BAHAMAS

avana

CUBA

Classic Car

Yacht

Loggerhead Turtle

DOMINICAN REPUBLIC

West Indies

JAMAICA

Port-au-Prince
HAITI

Santo Domingo

Kingston

ST. KITTS AND NEVIS

ANTIGUA AND BARBUDA

DOMINICA

Coral Reef

CARIBBEAN SEA

ST. LUCIA

ST. VINCENT AND THE GRENADINES

BARBADOS

Scuba Diver

GRENADA

Container Ship

Port of Spain

TRINIDAD AND TOBAGO

Panama Canal

Panama City

ANAMA

GULF OF PANAMA

The islands in the Caribbean have sandy beaches, warm seas, and coral reefs. It's the perfect place to scuba dive.

Dive underground

Dotted around Mexico's coast are thousands of underground caves and tunnels full of water. You're about to go cave diving, so stay close to the guide, who will show you the way.

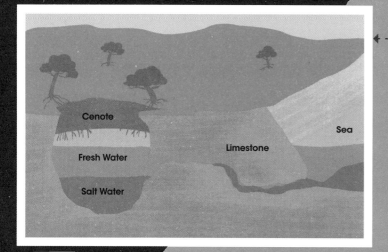

Cenote

Fresh Water

Salt Water

Limestone

Sea

Underground caves, called cenotes, form when the roof of a limestone cave collapses. Fresh water draining from the ground above sits on top of the salt water from the sea.

? What is the height of each stalagmite?

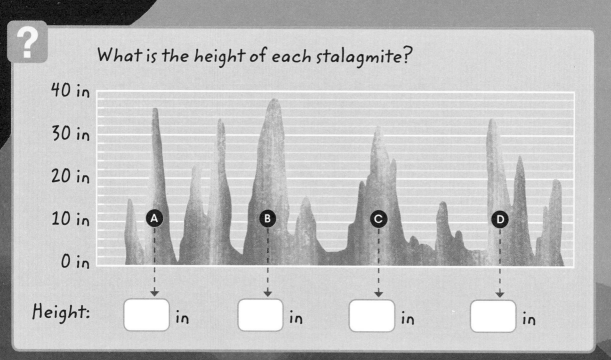

40 in
30 in
20 in
10 in
0 in

Ⓐ Ⓑ Ⓒ Ⓓ

Height: ☐ in   ☐ in   ☐ in   ☐ in

Many of the caves have amazing rock formations that look like icicles. Stalactites hang down from the ceiling. Stalagmites grow up from the floor.

Stalactites form when water drips from the roof of a cave. Minerals in the water are left behind and harden. Over time, more and more minerals build up.

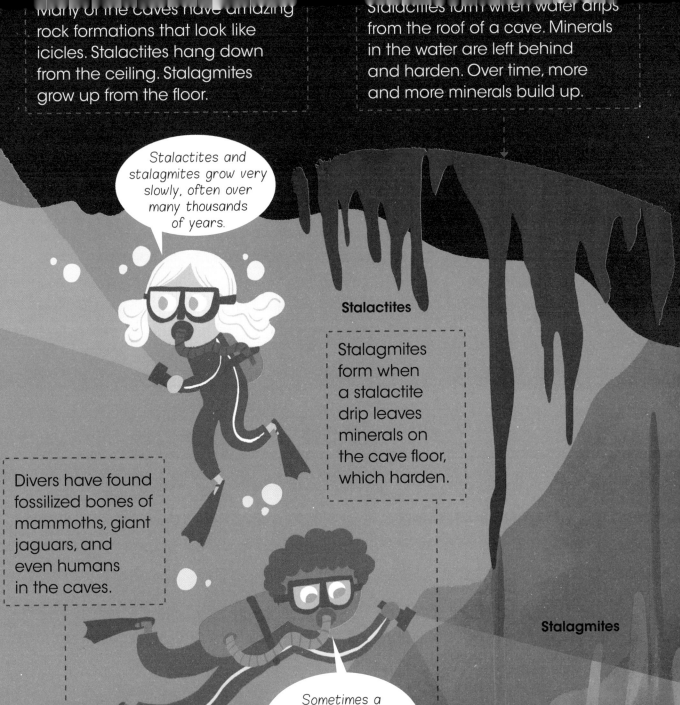

Stalactites and stalagmites grow very slowly, often over many thousands of years.

Stalactites

Stalagmites form when a stalactite drip leaves minerals on the cave floor, which harden.

Divers have found fossilized bones of mammoths, giant jaguars, and even humans in the caves.

Stalagmites

Sometimes a stalactite and stalagmite meet to form a long column of stone.

Navigate a canal

The Panama Canal goes right across Panama, linking the Atlantic and Pacific oceans. It's an important shortcut for ships and an incredible example of what humans can build.

The Panama Canal opened more than 100 years ago, in 1914. More than a million ships have traveled through it since.

A ship enters the canal at sea level. It passes through a series of locks that raise it up.

ATLANTIC OCEAN

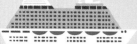

Ship enters the canal

A lock is a chamber of water with gates that open and close at each end.

Ships are lifted and lowered 85 feet in total. That's about the same height as a 9-story building.

Some very large ships have to pay hundreds of thousands of dollars to pass through the canal.

 Help the ship through the Panama Canal. Number these jumbled pictures in the correct order from 1 to 5.

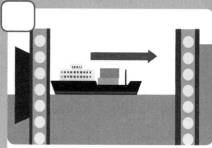

Water flows into the lock, lifting the ship up.

The ship enters the lock. The gates close behind.

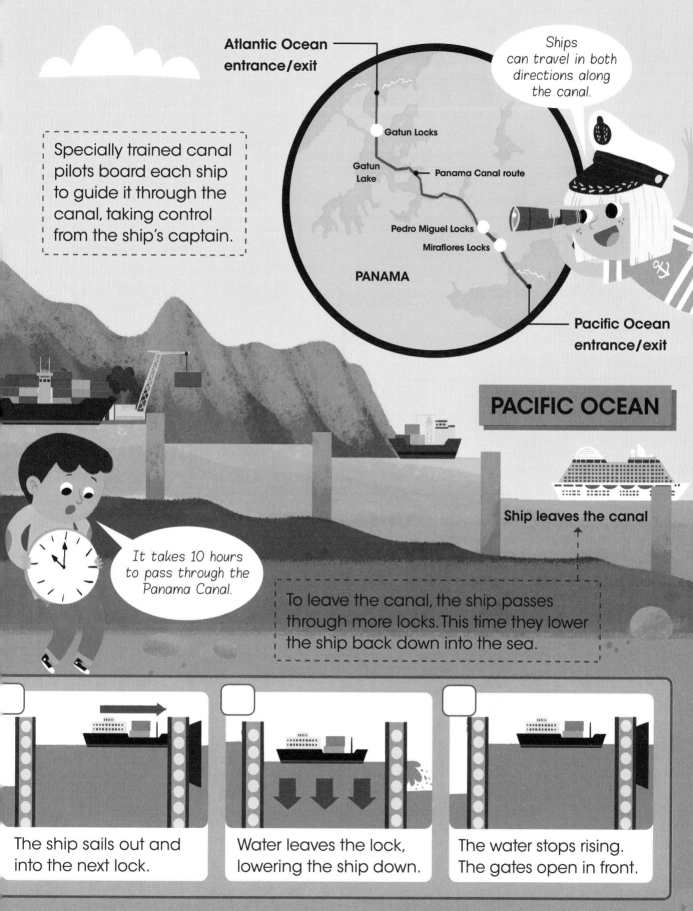

Atlantic Ocean entrance/exit

Ships can travel in both directions along the canal.

Gatun Locks

Gatun Lake

Panama Canal route

Pedro Miguel Locks

Miraflores Locks

PANAMA

Pacific Ocean entrance/exit

Specially trained canal pilots board each ship to guide it through the canal, taking control from the ship's captain.

PACIFIC OCEAN

Ship leaves the canal

It takes 10 hours to pass through the Panama Canal.

To leave the canal, the ship passes through more locks. This time they lower the ship back down into the sea.

The ship sails out and into the next lock.

Water leaves the lock, lowering the ship down.

The water stops rising. The gates open in front.

Spot a hurricane

You've arrived in the Caribbean. It's hurricane season and the weather is set to get seriously wild. Hurricanes start far out at sea, so get your binoculars out. Here's how you can spot when one's coming.

Tropical Storm

Depression

Thunderstorm

Frequent thunder and lightning

The storm starts to rotate

❶ Thunderstorm
Thunderstorms form when warm sea water heats the air above it. As the warm air rises, it carries water vapor that forms thunderclouds.

❷ Depression
The thunderclouds join together to form stormy clusters. This is called a depression. The depression grows higher and wider, with heavy rain.

❸ Tropical Storm
As the depression gets bigger and stronger, it starts spinning. The wind blows faster and faster, and the rain gets heavier and heavier.

Hurricane

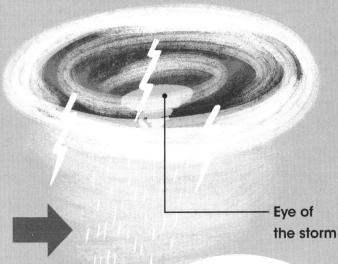

— Eye of
the storm

Hurricanes have eyes! The eye is the center of the storm where the wind drops and the sky is clear.

A hurricane can last for more than a week.

❹ Hurricane
The storm becomes a hurricane when the wind reaches 74 miles per hour. The hurricane is now about 120 miles wide.

Make a hurricane in a jar.

You will need:

- Jar with screw-on lid
- Liquid soap
- Food coloring

Parent note: Food coloring can stain. We recommend that precautions are taken to protect skin, clothing, and furnishings.

❶

Fill the jar with water, leaving an inch gap at the top.

❷

Squirt in some liquid soap and add a drop of food coloring. Screw the lid on tight.

❸

Swirl the jar with a circular motion for a few seconds, then put it down. What do you see? Your own mini–hurricane! Now try to swirl the jar even faster. Can you see the eye of the storm?

South America

Are you ready to explore South America? It's an amazing place! You'll find bone-dry deserts, soaring mountains, volcanoes, grasslands, and ice. It's also home to the mighty Amazon—the biggest river in the world. A third of all the plants and animals on Earth live in the Amazon rain forest!

ATLANTIC OCEAN

At almost 3,000 feet tall, Angel Falls is the highest waterfall in the world.

Equator

FRENCH GUIANA

Cayenne

Paramaribo

Georgetown

SURINAME

GUYANA

Angel Falls

Orinoco River

Caracas

VENEZUELA

Lake Maracaibo

CARIBBEAN SEA

Tatacoa Desert

Bogotá

COLOMBIA

Quito

ECUADOR

Tungurahua Volcano

PERU

Machu Picchu

A M A Z O N
R A I N   F O R E S T

Negro River

Amazon River

Tapajós River

Xingui River

Madeira River

A N D E

Toucan

Jaguar

SugarCane

Sao Francisco River

Brazilia Cathedral

Tocantins River

Galapagos Islands

Galapagos Tortoise

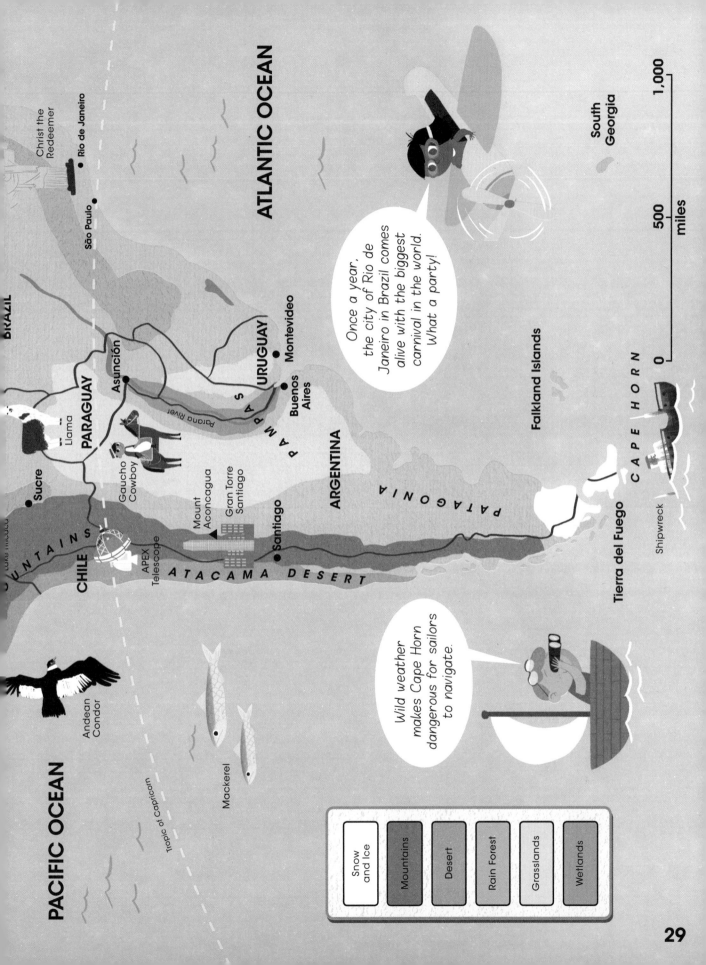

Trek the Andes

The Andes mountain range is the longest in the world. It's home to the ancient Inca ruins of Machu Picchu. Follow the historic stone paths of the Inca Trail that wind through the mountains and visit other Inca sites on your way.

Machu Picchu was built more than 500 years ago. There are more than 150 ruins of houses, as well as palaces, temples, farms, and homes to visit.

The Incas were skillful builders. Using simple tools, they cut huge stone blocks into shapes that fitted perfectly together.

I can't believe they got so much stone up here!

There are 3,000 stone steps to climb before you reach Machu Picchu.

Andean Condor

The Andes are home to some very rare wildlife, such as the Andean mountain cat. It has a long, bushy tail that can wrap around its body for warmth.

The Quechua people of the Andes are famous for their colorful costumes, which are woven from wool.

Here's a map of the historic Inca Trail. Which ruins will you see in each grid reference?

F6 _____   D4 _____

B5 _____   A3 _____

The ruins of Machu Picchu were lost until about 100 years ago.

| 1 | 2 | 3 | 4 | 5 | 6 | 7 | 8 | 9 |

A Machu Picchu

B Inti Punku

C

D Chachabamba — Intipata

E Phuyupatamarca — Winay Wayna

F Sayacmarca — Runkuraykay — START

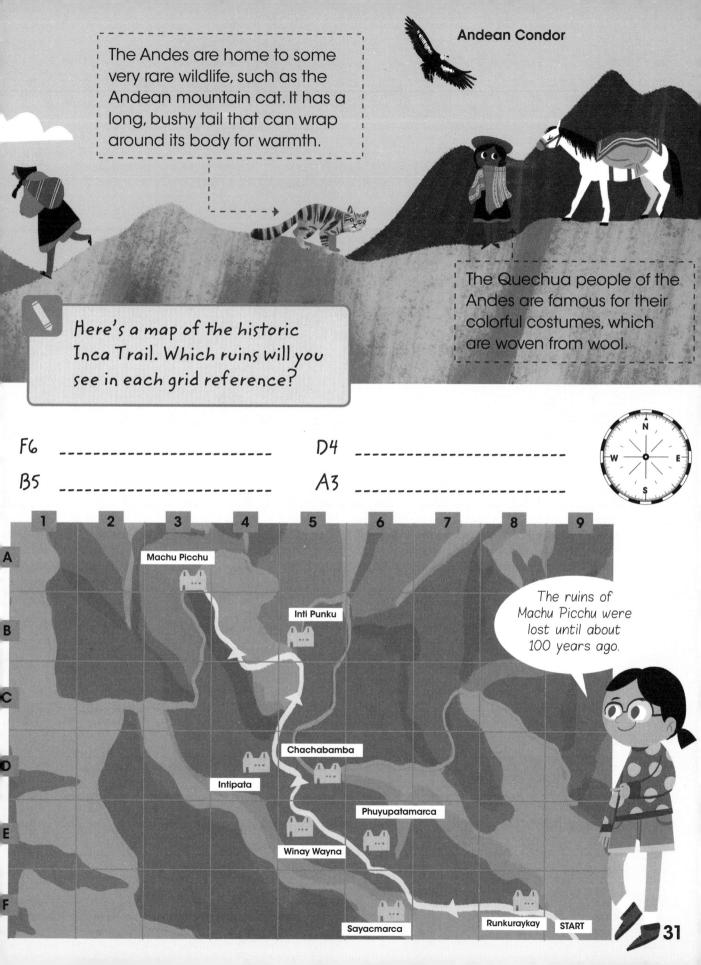

Canoe the Amazon

You've reached the enormous Amazon River, the biggest in the world. About 20 percent of all the river water on the planet flows through it. Enjoy your canoe trip, but watch out for dangers along the way!

Green Anaconda

Ooh, a green anaconda! Did you know it squeezes its prey to death?

sssssss!

Watch your fingers. These piranhas are hungry and might just take a bite!

SNAP!

SNAP!

Piranhas

Toucan

4,000 MILES LONG

Giant water lilies bloom on the river. They're so big and strong you could sit on them and not sink.

An area of Amazon rain forest the size of 2,000 football fields is chopped down every day. This destroys the habitat of the wildlife that lives there.

The Amazon rain forest is about the size of Australia!

It's home to around a million tribespeople, like us!

UP TO **25 MILES** WIDE

Spot the dangers and check each one off as you canoe past.

- ◯ Green anaconda
- ◯ Piranhas
- ◯ Waterfall
- ◯ Black caiman
- ◯ Poison dart frog

The Amazon River carries six times more water than any other river on Earth.

The black caiman has 75 long, sharp teeth to snap up fish and other prey.

MORE THAN **3,000** SPECIES OF FISH

SpLASH!

The poison dart frog is tiny but deadly poisonous. Its bright colors warn hungry predators not to eat it.

The boto is a pink dolphin that lives in the Amazon River. It hunts in the murky water, eating fish, shellfish, and even small turtles.

Botos leap out of the water and even swim upside down.

Meet a gaucho

Do you want to learn how to ride a horse and throw a lasso? Then spend the day with a gaucho—a cowboy or girl from the rolling grasslands of Argentina.

Yeehaw!

START ➡

A DAY IN THE LIFE OF A GAUCHO

Gauchos are expert horse riders. Their job is to round up and direct the cattle by galloping alongside and catching any strays.

I use a rope with a loop to lasso the stray cattle.

On hot afternoons, I siesta, or nap, in a hammock.

Find a way through the maze to the pen at the finish.
Round up all the stray cattle along the route.

Don't forget your cowboy hat!

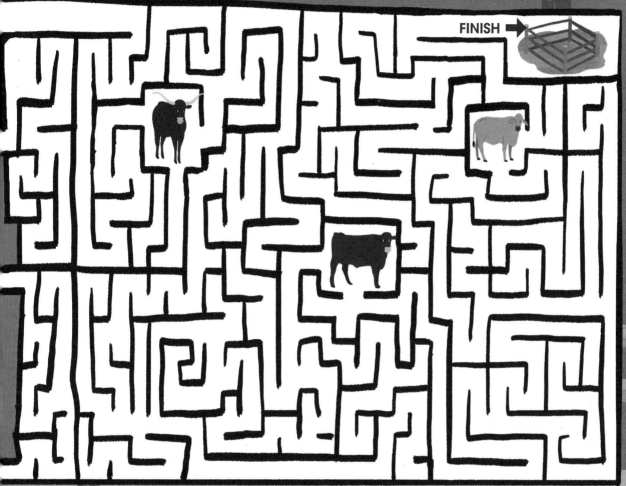

FINISH ➡️

AT THE RODEO

A rodeo is a competition where gauchos ride horses and show off their skills by lassoing and handling cattle.

I wear traditional clothes, including leather leggings called chaps.

When I ride a bucking bronco I can only hold on with one hand!

The Arctic

You've arrived in the Arctic Circle, an imaginary line circling the top of the globe. It's so cold here, the Arctic Ocean is frozen into an enormous area of ice. Amazingly, many types of animal call this freezing place home.

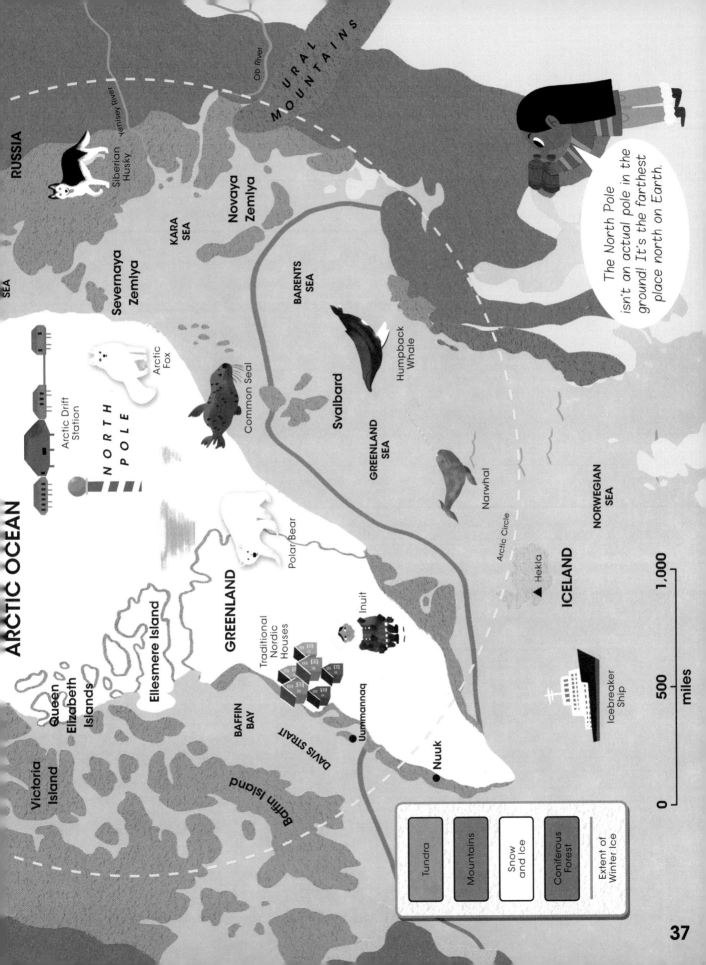

ARCTIC OCEAN

The North Pole isn't an actual pole in the ground! It's the farthest place north on Earth.

RUSSIA

Siberian Husky

Yenisey River

Ob River

URAL MOUNTAINS

SEA

KARA SEA

Severnaya Zemlya

Novaya Zemlya

BARENTS SEA

Arctic Fox

Common Seal

Svalbard

Humpback Whale

GREENLAND SEA

Narwhal

Arctic Circle

NORWEGIAN SEA

Hekla

ICELAND

Arctic Drift Station

NORTH POLE

Polar Bear

Queen Elizabeth Islands

Ellesmere Island

GREENLAND

Traditional Nordic Houses

Inuit

Icebreaker Ship

Victoria Island

Baffin Island

BAFFIN BAY

DAVIS STRAIT

Uummannaq

Nuuk

0   500   1,000

miles

Tundra

Mountains

Snow and Ice

Coniferous Forest

Extent of Winter Ice

Go tracking

During the Arctic winter, snow and ice covers the rocky ground that surrounds the frozen ocean, and nothing much grows. Despite this, many animals survive here. Let's follow their prints and track some of them down.

Find each animal's trail of footprints, then draw more footprints to join each track back up with the animal.

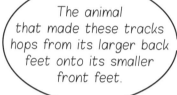

The animal that made these tracks hops from its larger back feet onto its smaller front feet.

Caribou

A caribou, or reindeer, eats lichen and moss hidden under the snow. It uses its hooves to dig down.

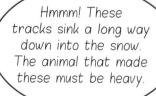

Hmmm! These tracks sink a long way down into the snow. The animal that made these must be heavy.

38

The polar bear has a chunky layer of fat beneath its skin and a thick layer of fur on top to keep it warm.

Polar Bear

An adult polar bear is very heavy. It has enormous paws that help spread its weight and stop it sinking too far into the snow.

These prints are small and are spaced quite far apart. They probably belong to a large animal with hooves.

An Arctic hare has a gray coat in summer to match the rocky ground. In winter, the coat turns white to blend in with the snow.

Arctic Hare

Build an igloo

Igloo is the Inuit word for home.

The Inuit people, who live in the Arctic, are experts at surviving in the cold. Help them build an igloo shelter out of blocks of snow.

1 Find a flat patch of firm snow. Using a knife or saw, cut about 30 large blocks.

It takes about an hour to build an igloo.

You need warm clothes in the Arctic. Traditionally, Inuits made their clothes from warm animal fur. Today, they usually wear man-made materials.

How can a house made of snow keep you warm?

Keep building! You'll find out later on ...

2 Lay a circle of blocks. Pack any gaps with snow.

3 Add more layers of blocks. Each time you add one, lean it slightly inward to make a dome.

4 Fit a final block tightly in the hole at the top. This makes the igloo strong.

The temperature inside an igloo can reach 60°F.

An igloo can keep you warm because it traps heat inside and helps keep cold air outside.

Now you just need to cut an arch for an entrance.

 Build a cloud dough igloo.

You will need:
- All-purpose flour
- Cooking oil
- A large bowl
- An ice-cube tray

1 Make cloud dough by mixing four parts flour to one part cooking oil in the bowl.

2 Make as many blocks as you need by pressing the mixture firmly into the ice-cube tray, then pushing out. There's no need to freeze or set the dough.

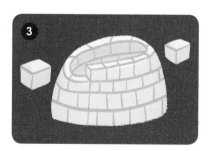

3 Make a circle of blocks and then build up the layers. You can press, cut, and shape the dough to help it fit together.

Drive a dogsled

Because the Arctic region is largely frozen over for most of the year, it's difficult to get about. People who live and work here mostly use snowmobiles to cross the ice, but they sometimes rely on sleds pulled by husky dogs.

Haw, haw—turn left!

Huskies can race along at speeds of up to 20 miles per hour: that's more than three times faster than a human child can run.

WOOF!

WOOF!

Huskies are used to pull sleds because they are tough and strong. They can run for hours across the ice without getting tired.

Up to 12 huskies can be used to pull a sled.

They've turned just in time to miss the crevasse!

HOW TO HITCH UP A SLED

1 Choose the strongest, most intelligent huskie to lead. It will set the pace and help find the best route across the ice.

2 Hitch the huskies in pairs. Attach their harnesses to the tug line that runs down the middle and back to the sled.

3 Hike! Hike!

Stand on the back of the sled and hold the line. Call **hike** to go, **haw** to turn left, **gee** to turn right, and **whoa** to stop.

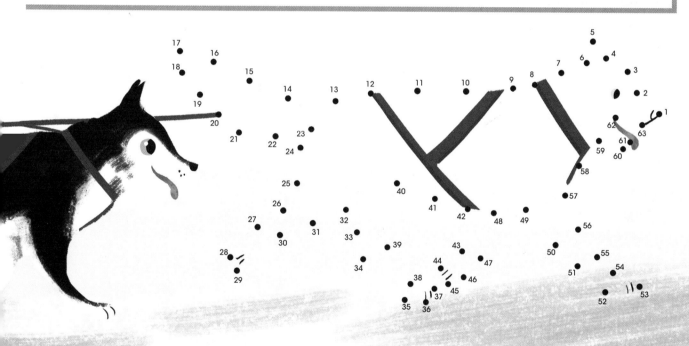

A crevasse is a crack in the ice. Some can be hundreds of feet deep.

Connect the dots to hitch up your lead dog. Then color it in.

Northern Europe

Let's explore Northern Europe—a part of the world that is steeped in history, filled with beautiful countryside, and home to many incredible cultures.

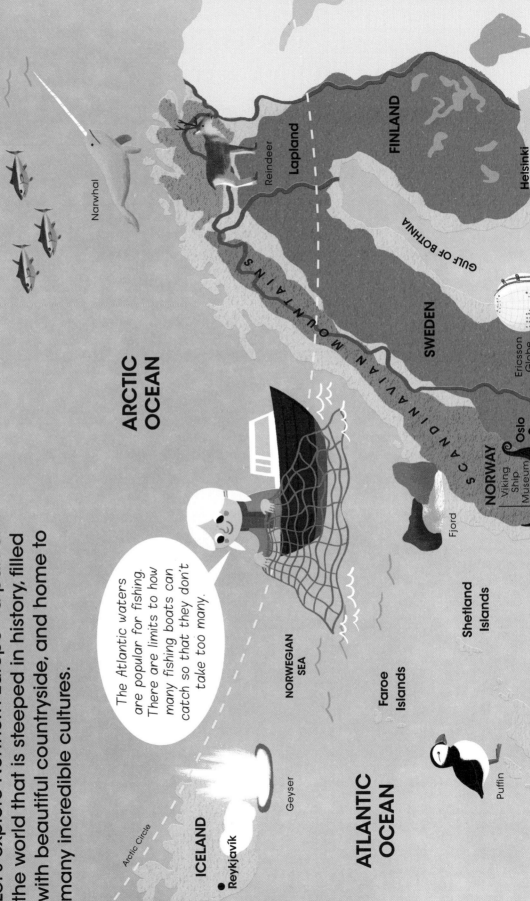

ARCTIC OCEAN

ATLANTIC OCEAN

NORWEGIAN SEA

The Atlantic waters are popular for fishing. There are limits to how many fishing boats can catch so that they don't take too many.

Narwhal

Reindeer

Lapland

FINLAND

Helsinki

OF FINLAND

GULF OF BOTHNIA

SWEDEN

Ericsson Globe

SCANDINAVIAN MOUNTAINS

NORWAY

Oslo

Viking Ship Museum

Fjord

ICELAND

Reykjavik

Geyser

Arctic Circle

Faroe Islands

Shetland Islands

Puffin

Northern

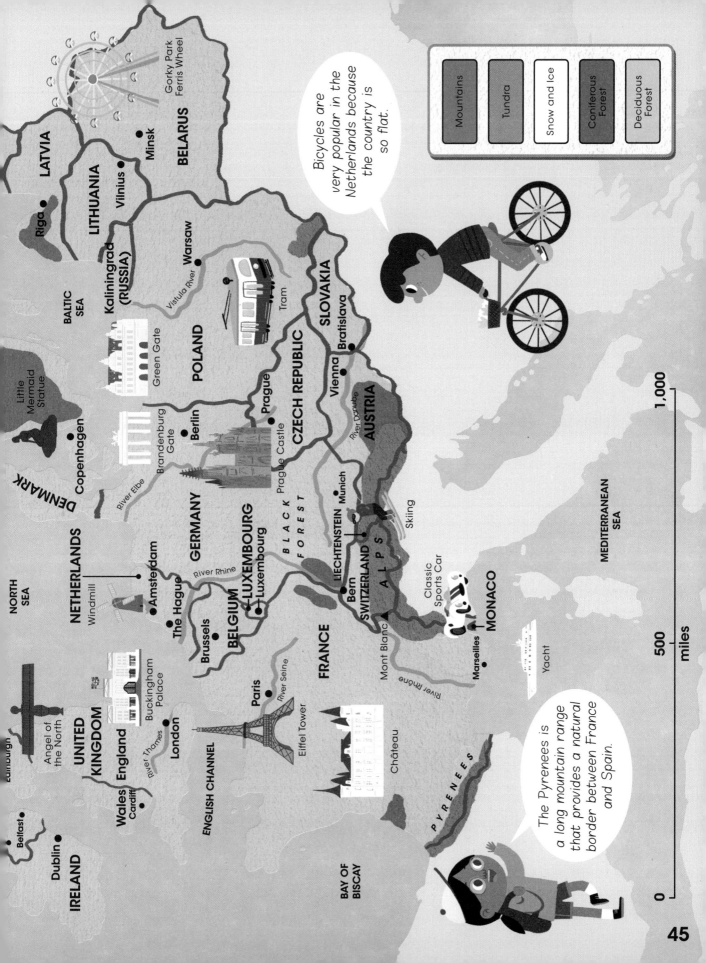

45

Stargaze in Lapland

It's winter in Lapland and you're going to spend some time with the local Sami people. The skies are often very clear, so you'll also have the chance to go stargazing and see the Northern Lights. Don't forget to pack some warm clothes.

Traditionally, Sami lived in cone-shaped tents, called kota, which were covered in reindeer skin to help protect them from the cold.

The Sami have kept herds of reindeer for more than a thousand years. Each year, they follow their herds to new supplies of grass and lichen, which the reindeer eat.

As well as herding reindeer, we hunt and fish too.

Traditional Sami clothing

Constellations are groups of stars that form a pattern. Sometimes the constellations are named after animals, such as a swan (Cygnus) or a bear (Ursa Major).

 Connect the dots to complete the constellations in the night sky.

Cygnus

Hercules

Ursa Major

Cepheus

You can use a telescope to take a closer look at the stars in the night sky.

The Northern Lights are a spectacular natural display of sweeping colors that appear in the sky around the Arctic Circle.

The Northern Lights are made by particles from the Sun passing through the atmosphere.

Ride the Métro

Bienvenue à Paris! Welcome to Paris! The best way to get around this beautiful city and its wonderful sights is by subway train on the Métro. Pick a line to follow and start exploring.

This monument's name means Arch of Triumph.

The Arc de Triomphe was built to remember French soldiers who died fighting for their country.

Arc de Triomphe

Place de la Concorde

Palai Garni

Trocadéro

Musée d'Orsay

Eiffel Tower

Jardin du Luxembour

You climb 1,665 steps to reach the top of the Eiffel Tower. Exhausting!

Roland Garros

Parc des Princes

The Eiffel Tower is the city's most famous landmark. Built in 1889, it is made from 12,000 pieces of iron.

River Seine

Montparnasse

Parc des Expositions

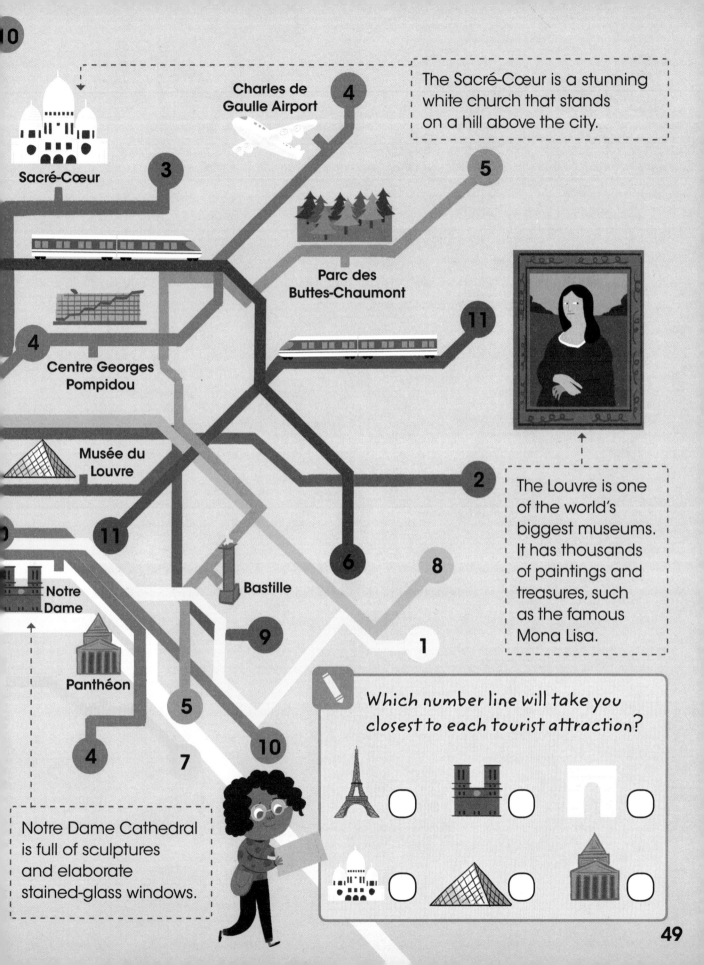

Charles de Gaulle Airport

4

The Sacré-Cœur is a stunning white church that stands on a hill above the city.

Sacré-Cœur

3

5

Parc des Buttes-Chaumont

11

Centre Georges Pompidou

4

Musée du Louvre

2

The Louvre is one of the world's biggest museums. It has thousands of paintings and treasures, such as the famous Mona Lisa.

11

Notre Dame

Bastille

6

8

Panthéon

9

1

5

Which number line will take you closest to each tourist attraction?

4

7

10

Notre Dame Cathedral is full of sculptures and elaborate stained-glass windows.

Eye up the skyline

Your next stop is London—the capital city of England and one of the most famous cities in the world. You'd need years to explore it all, but you can start by spotting these well-known buildings on the London skyline.

Each capsule on the London Eye weighs about as much as five cars.

The most famous church in London is St. Paul's Cathedral. It replaced a church that burned down in the Great Fire of London in 1666.

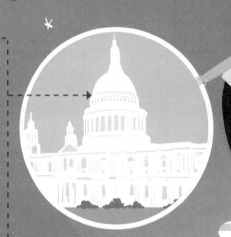

Tower Bridge crosses the River Thames. The bridge can be raised to let tall ships through. It opens hundreds of times a year.

Want a spin? For an unbeatable view of London, hop into one of the 32 rotating capsules on the London Eye.

A

B

The tall, thin pyramid shape of the Shard is the tallest building in London. If you're not scared of heights there's a viewing deck on the 72nd floor with spectacular views!

Match each letter in the skyline silhouette to a landmark.
◯ The Gherkin
◯ Big Ben
◯ The Shard
◯ St. Paul's Cathedral
◯ Tower Bridge

This building is nicknamed the Gherkin. Can you see why? It's covered in over 700 panes of glass.

Big Ben is a huge bell inside the clock tower at the Palace of Westminster.

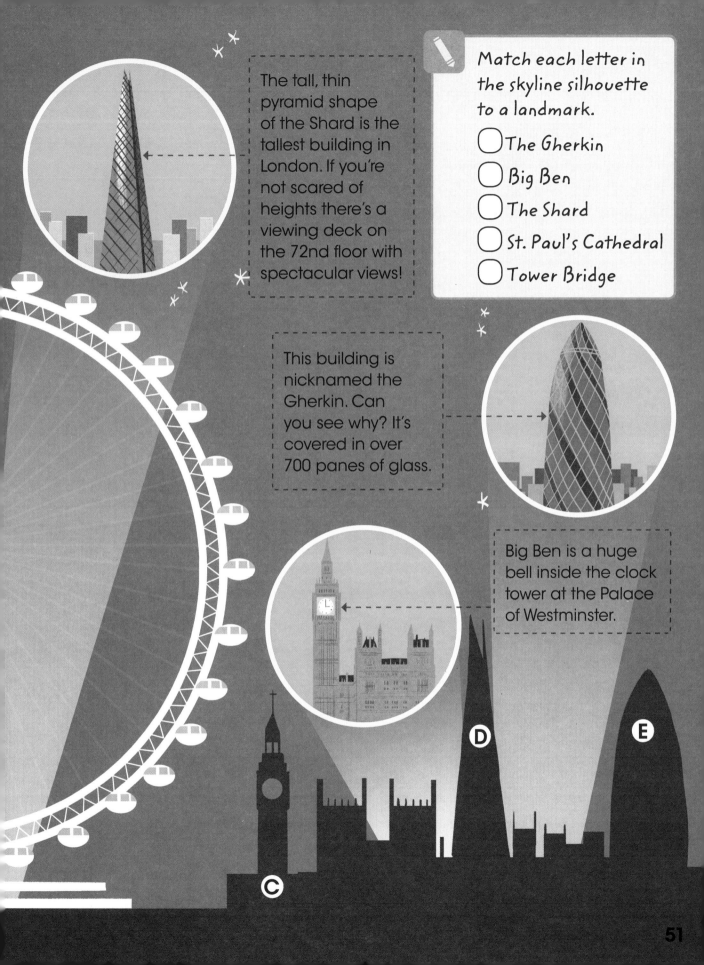

C

D

E

Southern Europe

Welcome to southern Europe! In the summer the weather is warm and sunny and some of the world's most popular vacation destinations are found here. Let's be tourists and discover some incredible things.

The Alps have some of the highest mountains in Europe and are very popular with hikers and skiers.

Fishing Trawler

ATLANTIC OCEAN

BAY OF BISCAY

Cave of Altamira

Paraglider

Skier

ALPS

Mont Blanc

Gond

Ven

Po River

PORTUGAL

Douro River

Ebro River

P Y R E N E E S

Andorra la Vella ● ━━ **ANDORRA**

Tower of Pisa

A P E N N I

● Lisbon

Madrid ●

Tagus River

● Barcelona

Casa Batlló

Corsica

VATICAN C

Ron

SPAIN

Colosse

Flamenco Dancer

● Gibraltar (UK)

Balearic Islands

Sardinia

| Mountains | Deciduous Forest |
| Wetlands | Coniferous Forest |

0   500   1,000
miles

Southern Europe has a strong tradition of dancing. Many countries have their own traditional dances that are still performed today.

Mountaineer

Gray Wolf

Kiev

Dnieper River

UKRAINE

Cossack Dancer

SEA OF AZOV

CARPATHIAN MOUNTAINS

MOLDOVA

Chisinau

Crimea

SLOVENIA

Budapest

ROMANIA

HUNGARY

Ljubljana Zagreb

CROATIA

Bran Castle

BLACK SEA

Bucharest

BOSNIA-HERZEGOVINA

Belgrade

RINO

Sarajevo

SERBIA

Danube River

ADRIATIC SEA

Sofia

BULGARIA

Podgorica Kosovo

MONTENEGRO

RHODOPE MOUNTAINS

Greece is known for its ancient ruins, such as the Parthenon temple.

ITALY

Skopje

MACEDONIA

Tirana

ALBANIA

Pizza

Pine Forest

GREECE

Yacht

Parthenon

Athens

Sicily

Mount Etna

MEDITERRANEAN SEA

Crete

MALTA

53

Take in a show

Have you ever been in a play or gone to see a show? Well here's where the idea of performing to an audience all began—in the ancient amphitheaters of Greece!

Ancient Greeks often spent the whole day watching plays, one after the other.

Amphitheaters are huge! Some of them had 18,000 seats. Important people sat at the front where they got the best view of the stage.

In ancient Greek theater, all the actors were men.

The actors wore masks to show which character they were playing. The masks had large mouths that made the actors' voices louder.

Some amphitheaters are still used today, even though they are ruins.

Music was often played as the actors performed.

 ## Make your own traditional Greek theater mask.

You will need:

- A balloon
- Strips of newspaper
- White glue
- A pen
- Paint and brushes
- Two lengths of ribbon

Parent notes: Warning! Children can choke or suffocate on uninflated or broken balloons. Adult supervision required. Keep uninflated balloons away from children and discard broken balloons at once. Paints and glue can stain. We recommend that precautions are taken to protect skin, clothing, and furnishings.

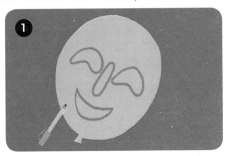

Blow up a balloon so it's about the size of your head. Draw on some eyes, a nose, and a large mouth with a pen.

Glue strips of newspaper into a mask shape, leaving spaces for the eyes and mouth. Add extra layers to make the mask stronger.

Build up the nose so it stands out by gluing on extra strips of newspaper.

When the mask is dry, pop the balloon and paint the mask a bright color.

Make a small hole on each side of the mask. Push the ribbons through and knot inside.

Tie the mask securely around your head. You are now ready to act in an ancient Greek play!

Hop on a gondola

The beautiful city of Venice in Italy is made up of more than 100 tiny islands, joined together by canals. There aren't any roads, so a popular way to see the sights is in a Venetian boat, called a gondola.

START

How do I get to the Doge's Palace?

The Grand Canal is the biggest and busiest canal in the city. Here you'll find many water buses and water taxis.

A gondolier stands at the back of the gondola and pushes the boat along with a long oar.

GRAND CANAL

The Turks' Inn

Pizza Shop

Gelato (Ice Cream)

Basilica di S. Maria Gloriosa dei Frari

GRAND CANAL

Ca' Rezzonico Palace

Grass Palac

Find the boy by the START sign above. Help steer his gondola to the Doge's Palace, avoiding bridges and other gondolas.

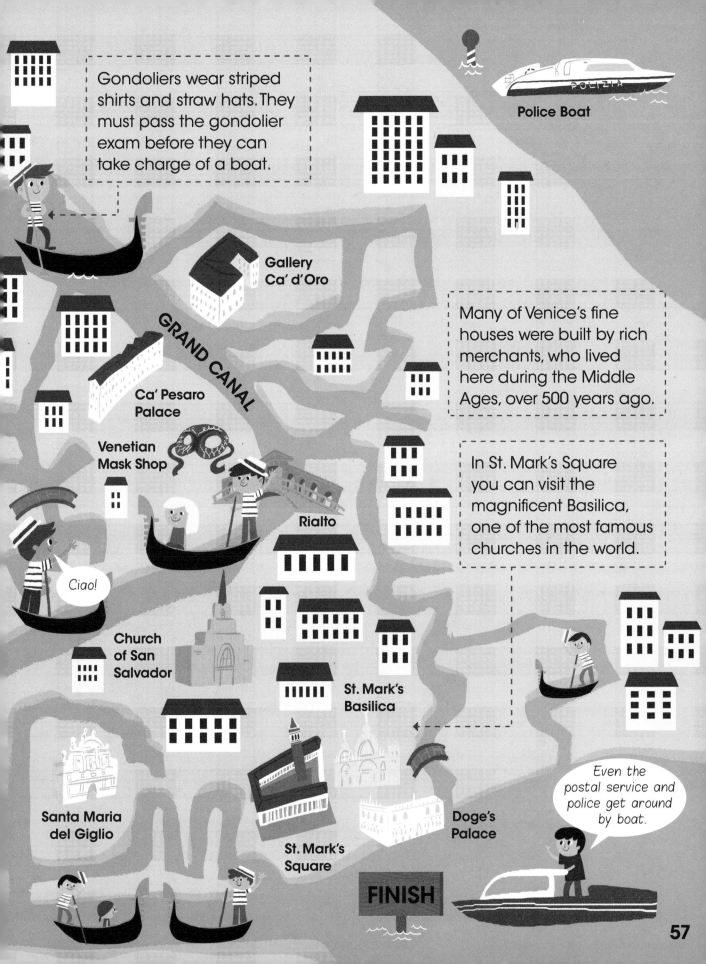

Gondoliers wear striped shirts and straw hats. They must pass the gondolier exam before they can take charge of a boat.

Police Boat

Gallery Ca' d'Oro

GRAND CANAL

Many of Venice's fine houses were built by rich merchants, who lived here during the Middle Ages, over 500 years ago.

Ca' Pesaro Palace

Venetian Mask Shop

Rialto

In St. Mark's Square you can visit the magnificent Basilica, one of the most famous churches in the world.

Ciao!

Church of San Salvador

St. Mark's Basilica

Santa Maria del Giglio

St. Mark's Square

Doge's Palace

Even the postal service and police get around by boat.

FINISH

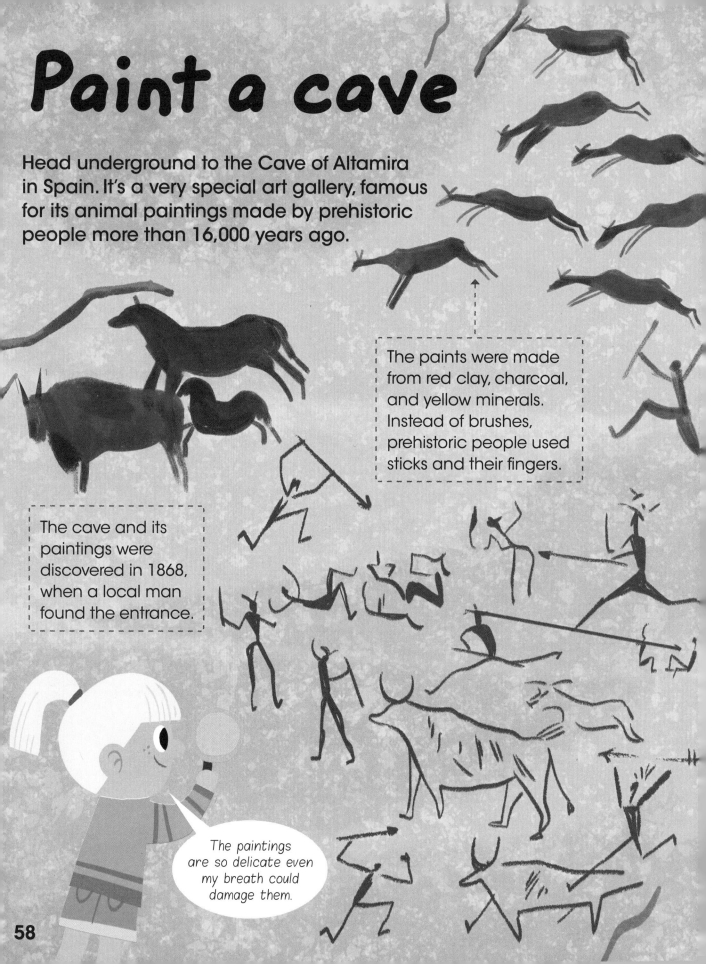

Paint a cave

Head underground to the Cave of Altamira in Spain. It's a very special art gallery, famous for its animal paintings made by prehistoric people more than 16,000 years ago.

The paints were made from red clay, charcoal, and yellow minerals. Instead of brushes, prehistoric people used sticks and their fingers.

The cave and its paintings were discovered in 1868, when a local man found the entrance.

The paintings are so delicate even my breath could damage them.

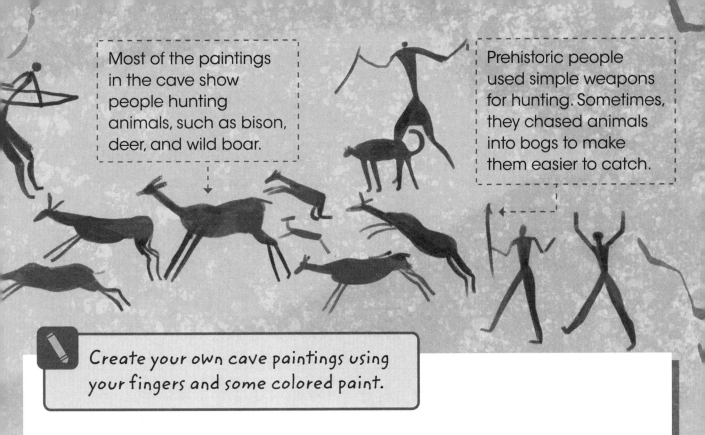

Most of the paintings in the cave show people hunting animals, such as bison, deer, and wild boar.

Prehistoric people used simple weapons for hunting. Sometimes, they chased animals into bogs to make them easier to catch.

Create your own cave paintings using your fingers and some colored paint.

Northern Africa

Your journey continues to the huge, sun-baked continent of Africa. Explore the world's biggest sandy desert, learn about ancient history, and track some of Africa's famous wildlife.

MEDITERRANEAN SEA

Hassan Tower

Algiers

Rabat ●
Casablanca ● MOROCCO

Algiers Cityscape

Madeira

Canary Islands

The massive Sahara Desert is about the size of the United States. Imagine all that sand!

Jebel Toubkal ▲ ATLAS MOUNTAINS

ALGERIA

M'zab

Tropic of Cancer

WESTERN SAHARA

Laâyoune ●

AHAGGAR MOUNTAIN

SAHAR

Dromedary Camel

MALI

CAPE VERDE

Nouakchott ●

MAURITANIA

River Niger

● Praia

Senegal River

Great Mosque of Djenné

Dakar ● SENEGAL

THE GAMBIA ● Banjul

Bamako ●

BURKINA FASO

Niamey ●

Bissau

Ouagadougou

GUINEA-BISSAU

GUINEA

BENIN

Conakry ●

GHANA

TOGO

Abu

Freetown ●

IVORY COAST

Lake Volta

Lagos ●

SIERRA LEONE

Yamoussoukro ●

Accra ● Lomé ●

ATLANTIC OCEAN

LIBERIA

Monrovia ●

Porto-Novo

Abidjan ●

GULF OF GUINEA

Blue Whale

Equator

| Mountains |
| Desert |
| Rain Forest |
| Grasslands |

0   500   1,000
miles

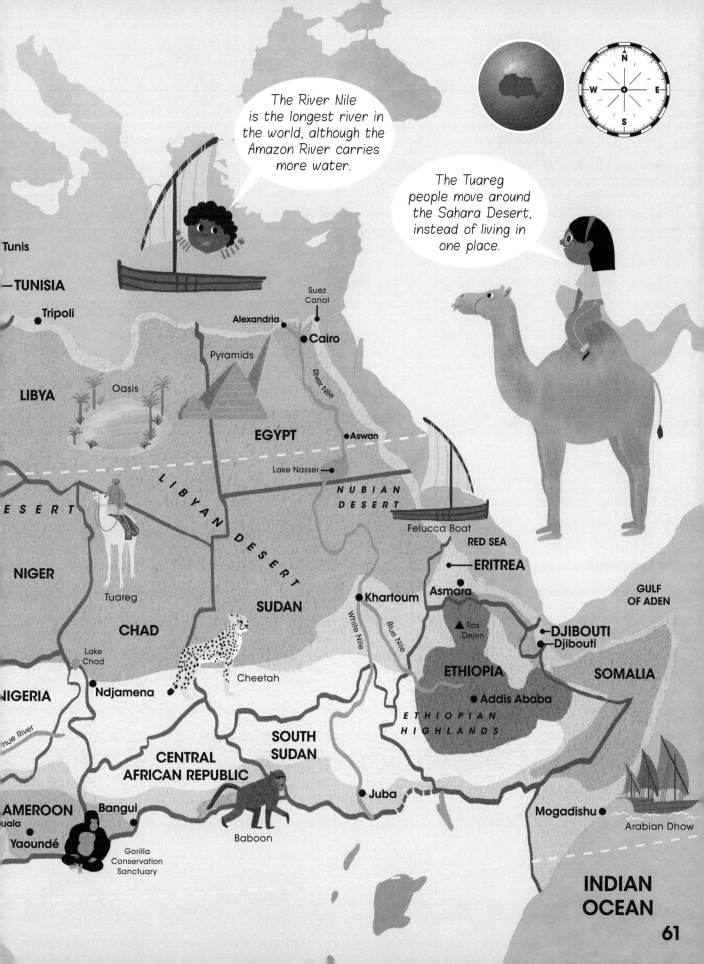

The River Nile is the longest river in the world, although the Amazon River carries more water.

The Tuareg people move around the Sahara Desert, instead of living in one place.

Tunis

—TUNISIA

Tripoli

LIBYA

Oasis

Pyramids

Alexandria

Suez Canal

Cairo

River Nile

EGYPT

Aswan

Lake Nasser

NUBIAN DESERT

Felucca Boat

RED SEA

ERITREA

Asmara

GULF OF ADEN

LIBYAN DESERT

DESERT

NIGER

Tuareg

CHAD

Khartoum

White Nile

Blue Nile

Ras Dejen

DJIBOUTI

Djibouti

SUDAN

Cheetah

Lake Chad

ETHIOPIA

SOMALIA

NIGERIA

Ndjamena

Addis Ababa

ETHIOPIAN HIGHLANDS

nue River

CENTRAL AFRICAN REPUBLIC

SOUTH SUDAN

Juba

AMEROON

Bangui

Mogadishu

uala

Yaoundé

Baboon

Gorilla Conservation Sanctuary

Arabian Dhow

INDIAN OCEAN

Trek the Sahara

Imagine trekking through the sweltering desert, stretching on forever in front of you. You're hot and thirsty. Suddenly you see something that looks like a shimmering pool of water in the distance.
But is it really water?

An oasis is a lush area of plants surrounding a spring or pool of water. There are about 90 real oases across the Sahara Desert.

I'm thirsty! Thankfully there's an oasis straight ahead.

Humans need water every day, so knowing where to find it in the desert is very important.

OASIS

The Tuareg people are expert guides to the Sahara Desert. They travel with herds of camels across the desert, but also have homes where they grow food.

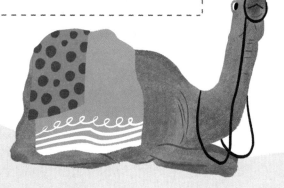

Sometimes people think they've spotted an oasis. but they're actually looking at a mirage!

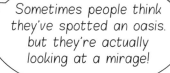

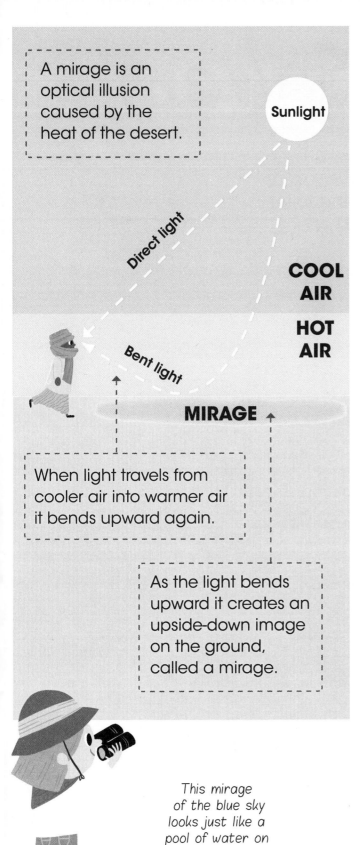

A mirage is an optical illusion caused by the heat of the desert.

Sunlight

Direct light

COOL AIR

HOT AIR

Bent light

MIRAGE

When light travels from cooler air into warmer air it bends upward again.

As the light bends upward it creates an upside-down image on the ground, called a mirage.

This mirage of the blue sky looks just like a pool of water on the ground.

Create your own mirage in a glass.

You will need:
- Two pitchers
- Water
- A glass
- Salt

①

Ask an adult to dissolve a few spoons of salt in some hot water in one pitcher. Let it cool, then half-fill your glass.

②

Put some cold water in the other pitcher. Slowly pour it on top of the salt water in the glass.

③

Look at an object through the glass. You should see a mirror image like a mirage. Each layer of water bends the light differently.

Explore a pyramid

Wow, the Great Pyramid of Giza—one of the famous Seven Wonders of the World! Built by the ancient Egyptians around 2560 BC, this was the tallest building on Earth for more than 3,800 years.

The Great Pyramid was built with more than two million blocks of stone. It was a tomb for the mummified body of the Egyptian king Pharaoh Khufu.

King's chamber

Ooh, ancient treasure! Many of the pyramid's valuables were taken by looters hundreds of years ago.

The Great Pyramid's chambers were linked together by tunnels.

The pyramid had three main chambers in which precious belongings, such as gold and jewelry, were buried alongside the king.

Underground chamber

The ancient Egyptians wrote using pictures, called hieroglyphs, instead of letters of the alphabet. Each picture stood for a different sound.

Decode the hieroglyphic message, then answer the question.

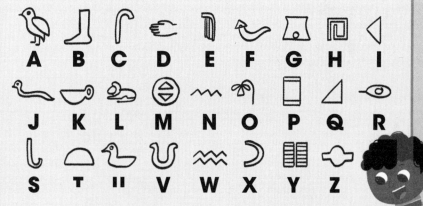

A B C D E F G H I
J K L M N O P Q R
S T U V W X Y Z

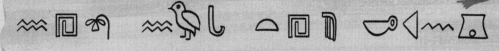

___ ___ ___ ___?

Answer: _____

Air shaft

Grand gallery

Queen's chamber

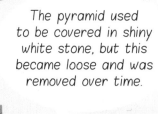

The pyramid used to be covered in shiny white stone, but this became loose and was removed over time.

The grand gallery was a 27-foot high room leading to the king's chamber. It was sealed at both ends with granite blocks to protect the tomb from raiders.

Find gorillas

Gorillas live deep in forests, so finding these awesome apes isn't easy. But once you've tracked them down you'll be amazed by the mighty adult males, caring mommies, and playful infants.

An adult male gorilla can eat 65 pounds of leaves and fruit in one day—similar to you munching through 140 apples!

Gorillas build nests. They find a spot on the ground or in a tree and tuck leaves and branches around themselves.

Gorillas are in danger. Their forest home is being cut down and some are being killed by hunters.

VIEWING PLATFORM

No flash photography please

Gorillas have powerful arms and tough hands to help them climb and swing through the trees.

Check off each telltale sign of gorillas you can find in the picture.

Broken plants ◯
Prints ◯
Nests ◯
Dung ◯

Sometimes, the silverbacks fight to work out who is in charge of the group.

Gorillas live in troops, with one or two older males, called silverbacks, and up to ten females plus their young.

Male gorillas are very protective of their troop, so we're staying a safe distance away.

Southern Africa

At the heart of southern Africa is a massive area of grassland about the size of India. To the east is the large island of Madagascar, home to an incredible number of animals and plants that are found nowhere else on Earth.

The Congo rain forest acts like a lung for the world, taking carbon dioxide from the air and giving out oxygen for us to breathe.

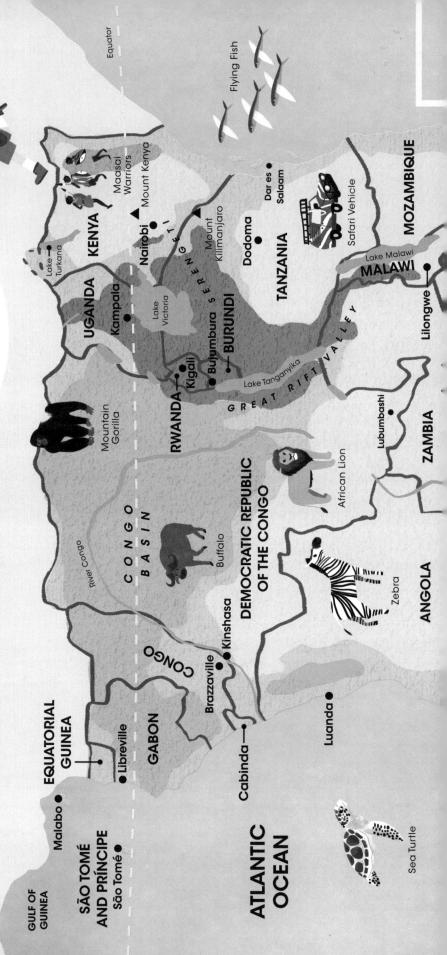

Equator

Flying Fish

MOZAMBIQUE

Maasai Warriors

Mount Kenya

KENYA

Dar es Salaam

Safari Vehicle

Nairobi

Dodoma

TANZANIA

Lake Malawi

MALAWI

Lilongwe

Lake Turkana

UGANDA

Kampala

S E R E N G E T I

Lake Victoria

BURUNDI

Bujumbura

Lake Tanganyika

Kigali

RWANDA

G R E A T   R I F T   V A L L E Y

Lubumbashi

ZAMBIA

Mountain Gorilla

African Lion

DEMOCRATIC REPUBLIC OF THE CONGO

Zebra

ANGOLA

River Congo

C O N G O   B A S I N

Buffalo

CONGO

Kinshasa

Brazzaville

Luanda

Cabinda

EQUATORIAL GUINEA

Libreville

GABON

GULF OF GUINEA

Malabo

SÃO TOMÉ AND PRÍNCIPE

São Tomé

ATLANTIC OCEAN

Sea Turtle

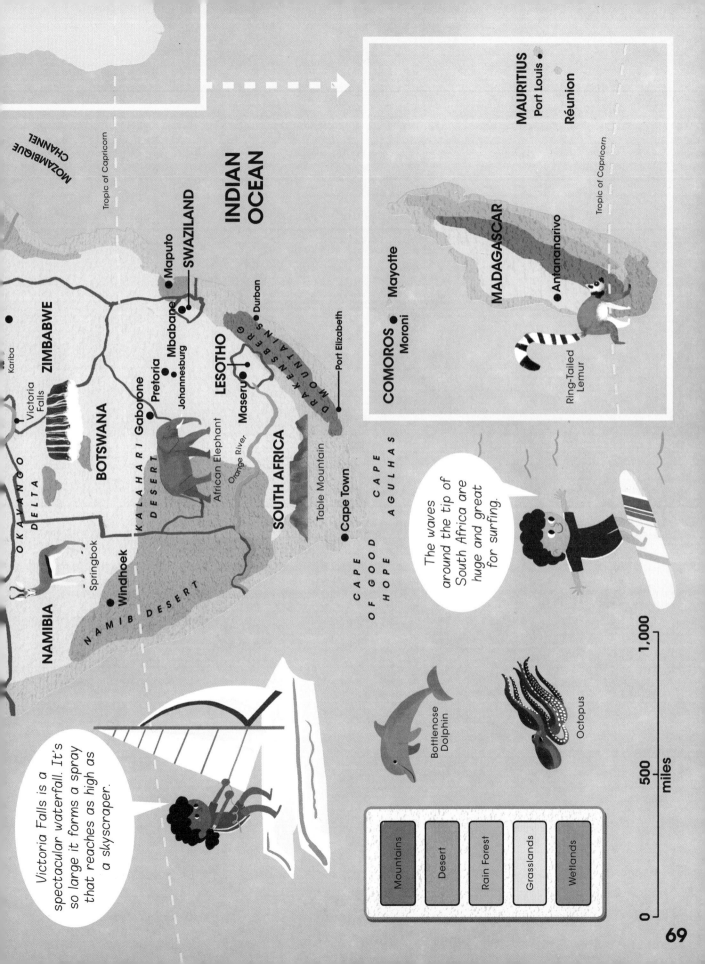

MOZAMBIQUE CHANNEL

Tropic of Capricorn

MAURITIUS
Port Louis •

Réunion •

Tropic of Capricorn

INDIAN OCEAN

MADAGASCAR

COMOROS •
Moroni

Mayotte

Antananarivo •

Ring-Tailed Lemur

ZIMBABWE

Kariba

Victoria Falls

• Maputo
SWAZILAND

Durban •

BOTSWANA

KALAHARI Gaborone
DESERT

Pretoria •
Mbabane •
Johannesburg •

LESOTHO

Maseru •

DRAKENSBERG MOUNTAINS

Port Elizabeth •

OKAVANGO DELTA

African Elephant

Orange River

SOUTH AFRICA

Table Mountain

NAMIBIA

Springbok

• Windhoek

NAMIB DESERT

• Cape Town

CAPE OF GOOD HOPE

CAPE AGULHAS

The waves around the tip of South Africa are huge and great for surfing.

Victoria Falls is a spectacular waterfall. It's so large it forms a spray that reaches as high as a skyscraper.

Bottlenose Dolphin

Octopus

Mountains

Desert

Rain Forest

Grasslands

Wetlands

0   500   1,000

miles

69

Go on safari

You're high above the grasslands of the Serengeti in Tanzania—what a view! The habitat is rich with incredible wildlife, so there's no better place for a safari.

Rhinoceroses

Giraffes are the tallest animals on Earth. They use their very long necks to reach food other animals can't.

Leopards

Pronghorns

Giraffes

Buffalo

Buffalo live in large herds. They move together as a way of protecting themselves from predators such as lions.

Lions sleep for about 20 hours each day. They save their energy for hunting, when they use their strength and power to take down prey such as buffalo.

Lions

How many of each animal can you spot from your balloon?

○ Elephants
○ Buffalo
○ Lions
○ Rhinoceroses
○ Pronghorns
○ Zebra
○ Giraffes
○ Leopards

We're approaching a watering hole, which all the animals rely on to survive.

Look at the giraffes. They're galloping just like horses.

African elephants are the largest land animals in the world. Their incredible trunks have about 100,000 muscles inside.

Elephants

Zebra

Herds of zebra travel across the grasslands. Their stripes merge together and make it hard for predators to single animals out.

Meet the Maasai

The Maasai people come from Kenya and Tanzania. They live in tribes and today keep herds of cattle, but traditionally they were brave warriors and hunters. You have been invited to spend a few days with them to learn about their life.

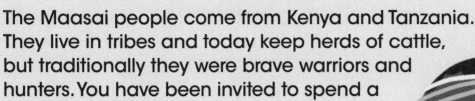

Young Maasai men take part in a special ceremony where they perform a jumping dance.

Headdress

Necklaces

The dance shows how fit and strong the young warriors are.

The Maasai live in villages, or engkangs, of around 10 to 20 small round huts. The huts are made from branches, mud, and grass and only have one or two rooms.

The Maasai like the color red because it represents strength and bravery.

Bracelets

Maasai people love jewelry. They make necklaces, headdresses, and bracelets using materials such as colorful glass beads.

Make your own Maasai shield.

You will need:

- Cardboard
- A pen
- Scissors
- Tape
- Paper
- White glue
- Paints
- Brushes

Parent note: Paints and glue can stain. We recommend that precautions are taken to protect skin, clothing, and furnishings.

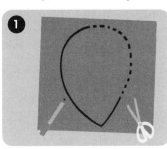

1 Draw a large leaf shape on the cardboard and cut it out.

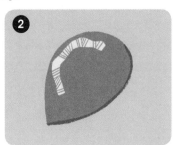

2 Roll up some paper and tape it to the back of the shield to make a handle.

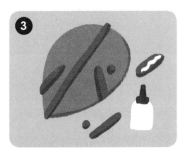

3 Cut out some cardboard shapes and glue them onto the front of the shield.

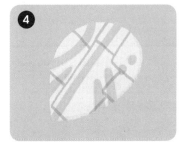

4 Cover the front of the shield with strips of torn paper using more glue.

5 Once the glue's dry, paint your shield using red, yellow, and orange paint.

6 Hold the shield using the handle, and try your own jumping dance!

Surf the Cape

The beaches around the Cape of Good Hope in South Africa are a surfer's paradise. Where the Atlantic and Indian oceans collide the result is plenty of waves. So pull on your wetsuit and grab your surfboard!

WIND

Lie on your board and paddle toward the shore until the waves start to break.

1 Waves start far out at sea. Energy from the wind causes the water to rotate (move in a circle).

2 As rotating water gets closer to the shore the water depth becomes shallower. This squashes the spinning water.

3 The sea floor slows the water at the bottom down. The water at the top starts to overtake.

Surfboards are made from foam and covered in a hard, protective layer called resin. This makes them light and strong.

Create your own cool surfboard design.

As a wave breaks, stand up on your board and try to balance while you're propelled toward the beach!

The breaking wave washes up the beach.

Water from previous wave washes back.

4 Finally, the faster water at the top of the wave breaks over the slower water at the bottom.

Surfboards often have bright pictures and designs on them.

North and Central Asia

Stretching right across North Asia is Russia, the biggest country in the world. It's nearly the size of South America! Central Asia is a region of deserts, mountains, and treeless grasslands called steppes.

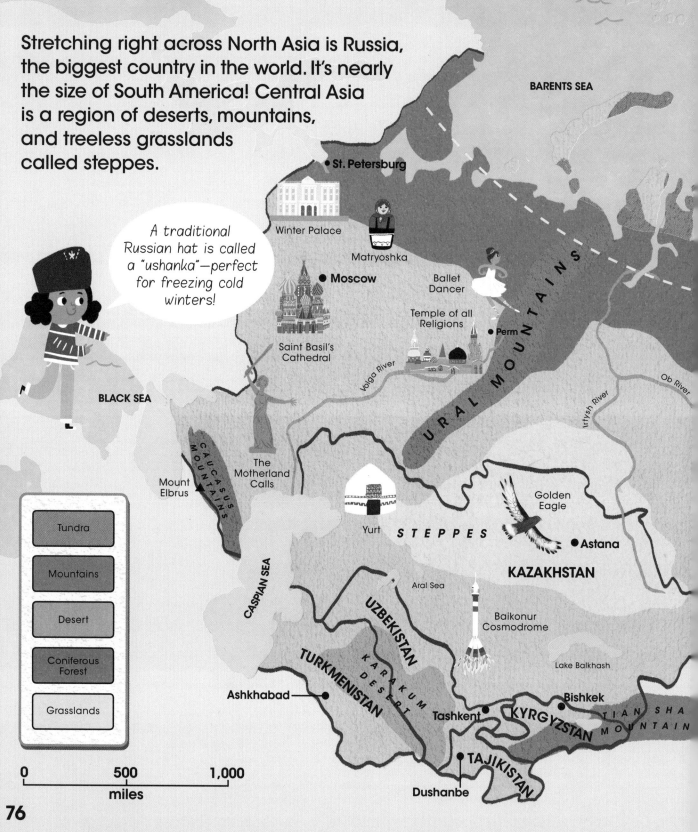

BARENTS SEA

St. Petersburg

Winter Palace

Matryoshka

A traditional Russian hat is called a "ushanka"—perfect for freezing cold winters!

Moscow

Ballet Dancer

Temple of all Religions

Perm

Saint Basil's Cathedral

Volga River

U R A L   M O U N T A I N S

Irtysh River

Ob River

BLACK SEA

CAUCASUS MOUNTAINS

Mount Elbrus

The Motherland Calls

CASPIAN SEA

Yurt

STEPPES

Golden Eagle

Astana

KAZAKHSTAN

Aral Sea

Baikonur Cosmodrome

Lake Balkhash

UZBEKISTAN

KARAKUM DESERT

TURKMENISTAN

Ashkhabad

Tashkent

Bishkek

KYRGYZSTAN

TIAN SHA MOUNTAIN

TAJIKISTAN

Dushanbe

Tundra

Mountains

Desert

Coniferous Forest

Grasslands

0   500   1,000
miles

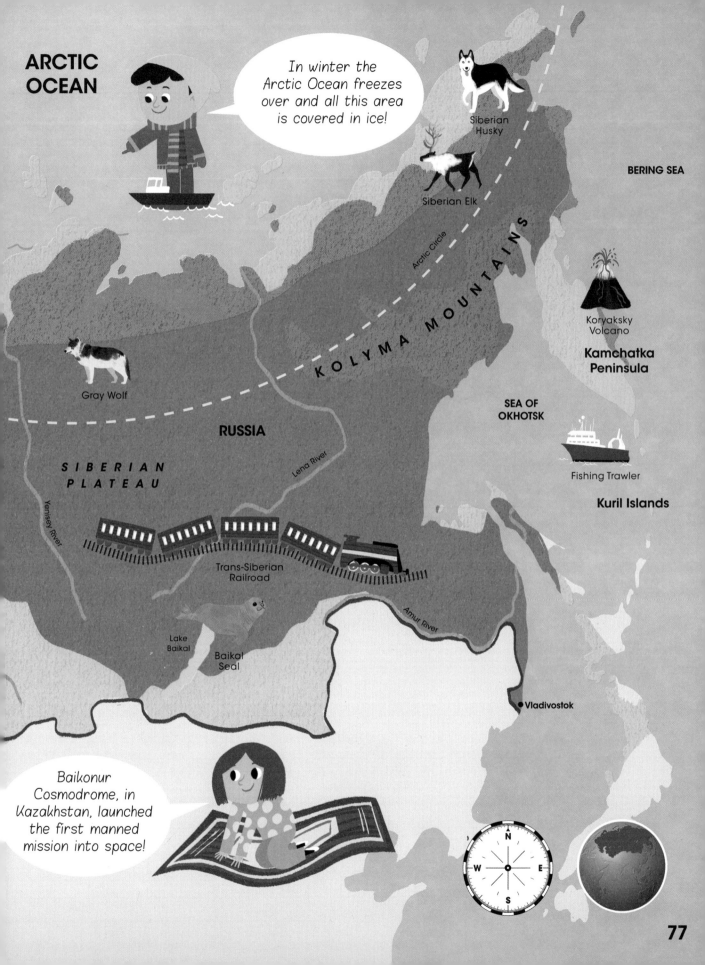

Camp in a yurt

Shanyrak

Traditional Kazakh people from Kazakhstan were nomads, moving from one place to another. They didn't build houses, but instead lived in sturdy tents called yurts. Here's your chance to spend a night in one.

Look, the top of the yurt is open, so you can see the sky.

Nomads played stringed instruments like this dombra.

Kazakh nomads used camels and horses to transport their yurt and belongings.

A yurt is a round tent with a domed roof. Its frame of wooden poles is covered in thick felt.

A traditional yurt is decorated with felt carpets called tekemets. Rugs hang on the walls.

Kazakh yurts have a pattern of wooden sticks in the opening at the top, called a shanyrak.

Kazakh nomads even traveled with their wooden furniture.

There is only one room in a yurt, and everyone shares the space.

A fire warms the yurt and the smoke escapes out of the shanyrak.

? The shanyrak appears in the center of the emblem of Kazakhstan. Can you spot which emblem is an exact match?

Emblem of Kazakhstan

A

B

C

Hop on a train

St. Basil's Cathedral in Moscow is over 450 years old.

The Trans-Siberian Railroad in Russia is the world's longest railway line, and it will carry you from one side of Asia to the other. The journey takes seven days, but how far will you travel?

Moscow

The towering domes of St. Basil's Cathedral were built to look like the flames of a bonfire rising up into the sky.

Moscow

Day 1 890 miles

Perm

Day 2 791 miles

Russia is famous for its ballet theaters, productions, and dancers.

Omsk

Day 3 386 miles

Novosibirsk

Day 4 1,147 m

Novosibirsk is the capital of Siberia, an enormous region in the center of Russia.

Perm

Perm Opera and Ballet Theater is one of the oldest and most respected in the country.

Novosibirsk

At Novosibirsk you can see huge sculptures at the city's famous snow and ice festival.

Irkutsk

The old wooden houses in Irkutsk are intricately and beautifully carved with suns, stars, birds, and trees.

The yellow route shows how far your train traveled on each day of the epic journey.

? Calculate how far you've traveled on your Trans-Siberian adventure, from Moscow to Vladivostok.

Total Journey: _____Miles

Khabarovsk

Day 6 1,441 miles

Day 7 475 miles

Arriving ships are often filled with new cars from nearby Japan and South Korea.

Irkutsk

LAKE BAIKAL

Day 5 628 miles

Chita

Vladivostok

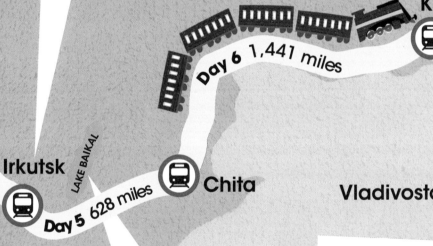

Lake Baikal

Lake Baikal freezes over in winter. It's older, deeper, and holds more water than any other lake in the world!

Vladivostok

Vladivostok is the end of the line, and is Russia's biggest port on the Pacific Ocean.

Visit a volcano

Kamchatka Peninsula, in the far east of Russia, is famous for its towering volcanoes, with more than 300 to explore. Many of them are still active, which means they could erupt at any time!

The highest volcano in Kamchatka is Klyuchevskaya Sopka. It's become taller over many years by erupting lava setting into rock at the top.

This volcano has a crater at the top, filled with water.

The water in Maly Semyachik's crater is light-green in color, due to a chemical called sulfur, which seeps up from inside the Earth.

Karymsky is the most active volcano in Kamchatka. It has been erupting regularly for at least 500 years.

Uka

Klyuchevskaya Sopka

Karymsky

Maly Semyachik

Khodutka

SEA OF OKHOTSK

Follow the key to color the picture and make the Karymsky volcano erupt.

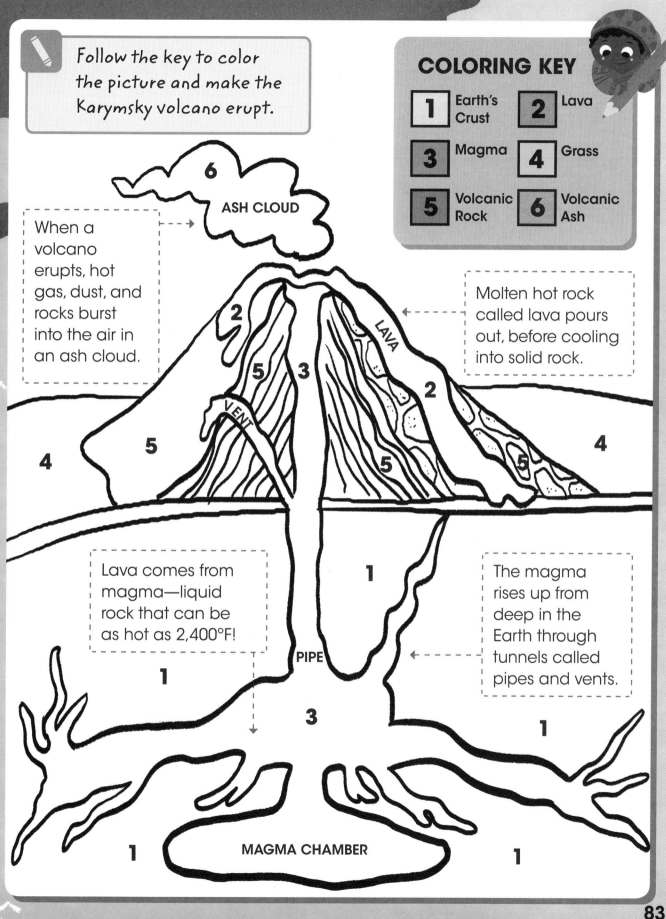

ASH CLOUD

When a volcano erupts, hot gas, dust, and rocks burst into the air in an ash cloud.

Molten hot rock called lava pours out, before cooling into solid rock.

LAVA

VENT

Lava comes from magma—liquid rock that can be as hot as 2,400°F!

PIPE

The magma rises up from deep in the Earth through tunnels called pipes and vents.

MAGMA CHAMBER

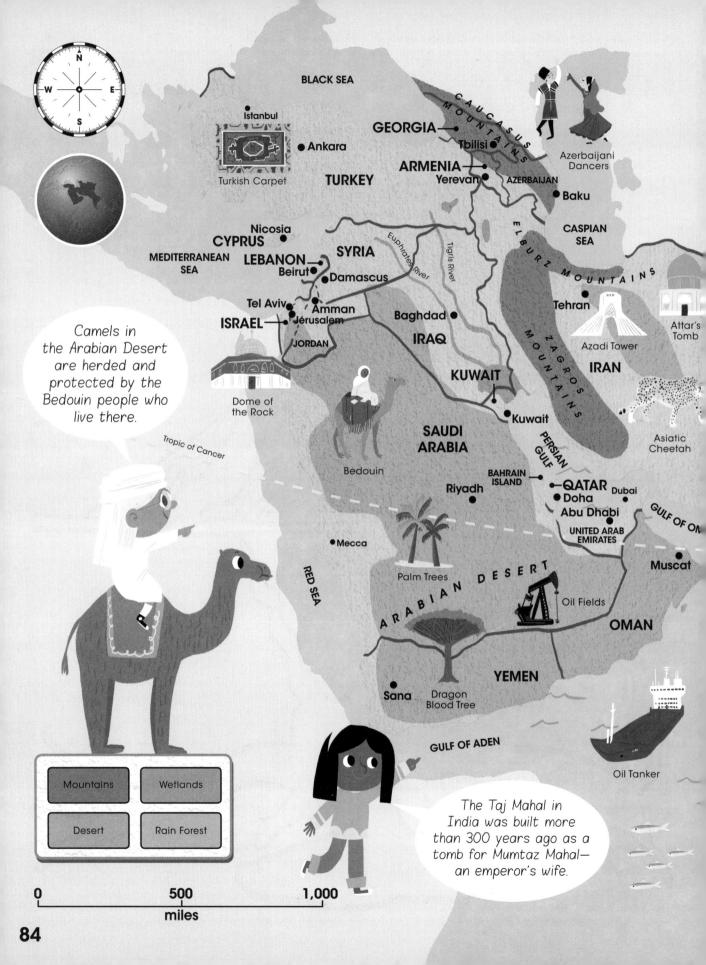

BLACK SEA

• Istanbul

Turkish Carpet

• Ankara

TURKEY

GEORGIA
Tbilisi

ARMENIA
Yerevan

CAUCASUS MOUNTAINS

AZERBAIJAN
• Baku

Azerbaijani Dancers

CASPIAN SEA

ELBURZ MOUNTAINS

• Nicosia

CYPRUS

MEDITERRANEAN SEA

LEBANON
Beirut •

SYRIA

• Damascus

Euphrates River

Tigris River

• Tehran

Azadi Tower

Attar's Tomb

ZAGROS MOUNTAINS

IRAN

Tel Aviv •

ISRAEL
• Jerusalem

Amman

JORDAN

• Baghdad

IRAQ

KUWAIT

• Kuwait

Asiatic Cheetah

Dome of the Rock

Camels in the Arabian Desert are herded and protected by the Bedouin people who live there.

Bedouin

SAUDI ARABIA

PERSIAN GULF

BAHRAIN ISLAND

QATAR
Dubai •
• Doha

• Abu Dhabi

UNITED ARAB EMIRATES

GULF OF OM

Tropic of Cancer

• Riyadh

• Mecca

RED SEA

Palm Trees

ARABIAN DESERT

Oil Fields

• Muscat

OMAN

Dragon Blood Tree

YEMEN

• Sana

GULF OF ADEN

Oil Tanker

Mountains | Wetlands
Desert | Rain Forest

The Taj Mahal in India was built more than 300 years ago as a tomb for Mumtaz Mahal— an emperor's wife.

0 — 500 — 1,000
miles

84

Middle East and India

The Middle East is hot and dry, with scorching, sandy deserts. Three of the world's great religions began here—Judaism, Christianity, and Islam. Traveling east, you reach the Indian subcontinent. It's a colorful and fascinating region of contrasts, from the soaring Himalayan Mountains to the wetlands of the mighty Ganges River.

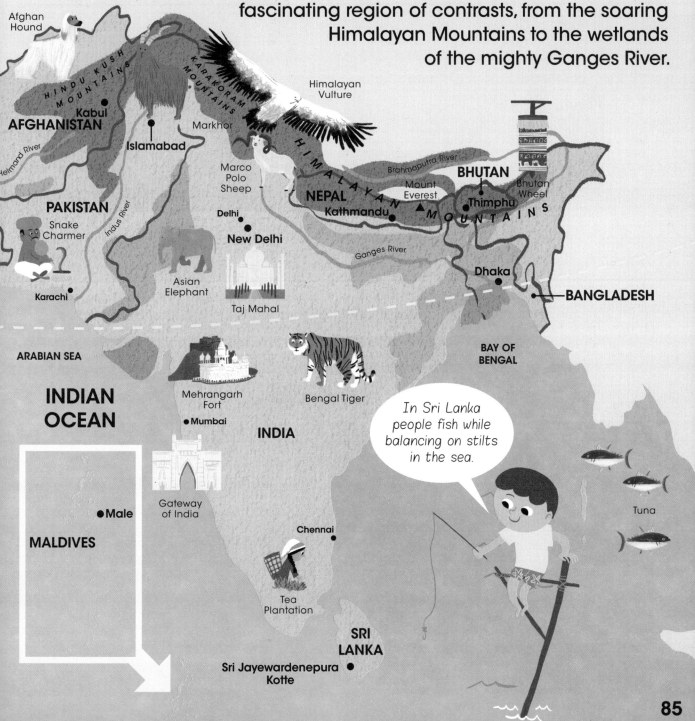

Afghan Hound

HINDU KUSH MOUNTAINS

KARAKORAM MOUNTAINS

Kabul

AFGHANISTAN

Markhor

Himalayan Vulture

Helmand River

Islamabad

HIMALAYAN

Marco Polo Sheep

Brahmaputra River

Mount Everest

BHUTAN

Bhutan Wheel

MOUNTAINS

PAKISTAN

Indus River

NEPAL

Kathmandu

Thimphu

Snake Charmer

Delhi

New Delhi

Ganges River

Asian Elephant

Dhaka

Karachi

Taj Mahal

BANGLADESH

ARABIAN SEA

Mehrangarh Fort

Bengal Tiger

BAY OF BENGAL

INDIAN OCEAN

In Sri Lanka people fish while balancing on stilts in the sea.

Mumbai

INDIA

Tuna

MALDIVES

Male

Gateway of India

Chennai

Tea Plantation

SRI LANKA

Sri Jayewardenepura Kotte

Race a camel

Here in the Arabian Desert, a day at the races can mean cheering on camels instead of horses. As the gate goes up, the camels thunder down the track, kicking up clouds of sand as they run. On your marks, get set, go!

Camels in the Arabian Desert are called dromedaries. They only have one hump.

Today, robots are used as jockeys. They're made to look like people and are dressed in colorful silks.

Camels can be quite stubborn. Sometimes there's nothing an owner can do to make their camel race!

People have been racing camels in the Arabian Desert for hundreds of years.

Today's robot jockeys are operated by remote control.

A camel's top speed is about 40 miles per hour—more than six times faster than you can run.

 Make and play this camel racing game with a friend.

You will need:

- Two sheets of cardstock
- Coloring pens
- Scissors
- A die

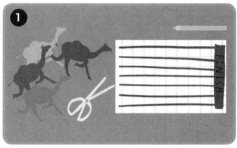

Draw six camels on one sheet, then cut them out. Color in and number them from one to six. Draw a grid with six rows and 10 columns on the other sheet.

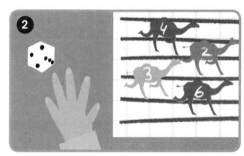

To play, choose three camels each. Place each camel at the start of its own row. Roll a die and move that number camel forward one space.

The first camel to cross the finish line is the winner.

Climb a mountain

Mighty Mount Everest in the Himalayas is the highest place in the world! Climbers from far and wide try to reach the top, avoiding the many dangers along the way.

SUMMIT
29,029 feet

ROCK FALL

Earthquakes can cause rock falls. Some boulders can be as large as a car.

CAMP 2

CAMP 3

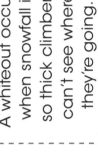

CAMP 3

WHITEOUT

A whiteout occurs when snowfall is so thick climbers can't see where they're going.

HIGH WINDS

CAMP 3

Strong winds as loud as a jet engine roar at the top of Everest.

CAMP 2

Avalanches are massive falls of snow that crash downhill, burying everything in their path.

AVALANCHE

CAMP 2

ICE FALL

Falling ice can block a route up the mountain in seconds.

CAMP 1

CREVASSE

Crevasses are giant cracks that can open up suddenly in the ice.

CAMP 1

CAMP 1

Climbers pitch camp higher and higher up the mountain, taking several days to reach the summit.

3 Ice picks help climbers grip and also test that areas of ice are safe to climb on.

Can you find a different route to the summit for each climber that passes through three camps along the way?

2 Eye masks help protect against the glare of the sun bouncing off the white snow.

1 Climbers wear special boots with crampons (spikes) attached to grip the ice.

BASE CAMP

Celebrate Diwali

Diwali is the Hindu festival of light, celebrated all over India and by Hindus around the world. It lasts for five days and is held in honor of the Hindu goddess Lakshmi, who is thought to bring luck in the following year.

People hang lots of lamps and candles around the home to celebrate hope and peace.

DECORATIONS

Colorful decorations of flowers, called garlands, are hung around homes and the streets where people live.

PATTERNS

Intricate and colorful patterns called rangoli are created on floors in the home.

CLOTHES

People wear new clothes to visit the temple, where they do puja, or prayers.

FIREWORKS

On the fifth and final day of Diwali there is a grand firework display to end the festival.

China and East Asia

Discover the treasures of this vast area, known as the Orient. It's a region of exciting contrasts between old and new, from the Forbidden City to the shiny skyscrapers of Hong Kong.

MONGOLIA

Eagle Hunter

ALTAI MOUNTAINS

GOBI DESERT

Urumqi

TIAN SHAN MOUNTAINS

TARIM BASIN

CHINA

TAKLAMAKAN DESERT

KUNLUN MOUNTAINS

The Tibetan Plateau is a huge area raised high above sea level. This is why its known as "the roof of the world."

Buddhist Monks

Yak

TIBETAN PLATEAU

Potala Palace

Panda

Brahmaputra River

Lhasa

Hkakabo Razi

Coniferous Forest

Rain Forest

Mountains

Desert

More than a billion people live in China—that's more than any other country in the world.

Mekong River

0   500   1,000
miles

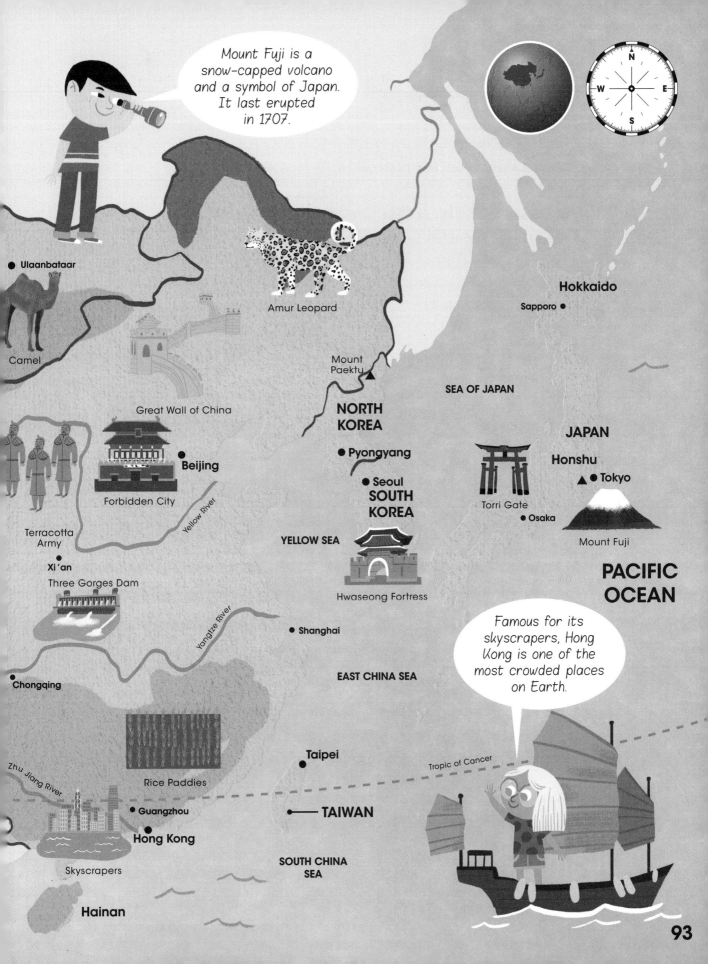

93

Walk the Wall

Parts of the Great Wall of China were built more than 2,000 years ago on the orders of Qin Shi Huang, the First Emperor of China, to keep enemies out of the country. Today, many parts of the Great Wall are still standing and you can even walk along them.

About 80,000 soldiers, prisoners, and slaves built the Great Wall over hundreds of years.

The Great Wall was built from earth, rubble, and rock, surrounded by a layer of stone bricks.

The wall is the longest structure ever built by humans!

Rice flour was used to fix the bricks together in some places.

STONE

EARTH

RUBBLE

ROCKS

MAPPING YOUR ROUTE

It would take a year and a half to walk all the way along the Great Wall.

Beijing

The Great Wall

CHINA

Thousands of watchtowers were built along the Great Wall. From here, guards could see far and wide.

If the guards spotted danger, they warned the next tower using fire, smoke signals, or flags.

The watchtowers are two stories tall. The first floor housed grain and weapons. The second floor was used for lookout points.

Battlements shielded guards from the enemy during an attack.

In some places stones have come loose and fallen out of the wall.

? True or false? Take the mini quiz!

TRUE FALSE

A. About 50,000 people built the Great Wall.

B. Guards signaled to other watchtowers.

C. The Great Wall was built to stop fierce animals.

D. Rice flour was used to make some parts.

Take some tea

In Japan, drinking tea is an important tradition and has its own ceremony. There are lots of special rules, so here's what to expect if you get an invitation.

The tea room is specially decorated. Straw mats cover the floor and delicate flowers add color to the room.

Lots of equipment is used in the tea ceremony. Each piece is precious, so it's looked after with care and always kept clean.

Guests kneel and wait quietly for tea to be offered.

The tea is kept fresh in a natsume, or tea caddy.

Natsume

Chashaku

THE JAPANESE TEA CEREMONY

1 The host arranges the equipment and adds matcha to the chawan.

2 The hishaku is used to tip hot water from the furo into the chawan.

3 The water and matcha is carefully stirred with the chasen.

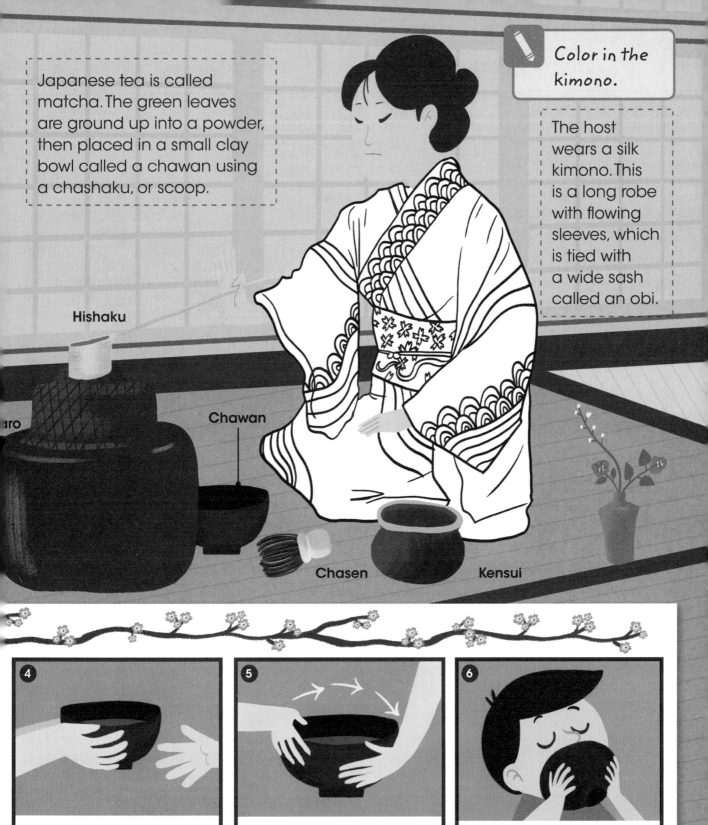

Japanese tea is called matcha. The green leaves are ground up into a powder, then placed in a small clay bowl called a chawan using a chashaku, or scoop.

Color in the kimono.

The host wears a silk kimono. This is a long robe with flowing sleeves, which is tied with a wide sash called an obi.

Hishaku

ro

Chawan

Chasen

Kensui

4 The host then places the chawan in the guest's right hand.

5 The guest rotates the chawan clockwise three times and drinks.

6 After drinking, the guest wipes the chawan, rotating it counterclockwise.

Dance with dragons

It's Chinese New Year—a 15-day festival and the most important in China's calendar. Homes are decorated with lanterns, and street celebrations are filled with dancing dragons.

In the Chinese calendar, every year is named after an animal. The animals each have different qualities.

It's believed you inherit the qualities belonging to the animal of the year in which you're born.

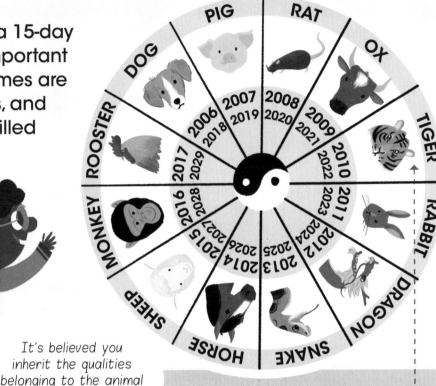

People born in the year of the tiger are said to be brave and powerful.

A team of skilled dancers holds the dragon model. The dancers walk and sway to make it look as if the dragon is moving.

Gong Hei Fard Choy! Happy New Year!

People draw the animal of Chinese New Year on lanterns. Using the dates on the wheel, draw the correct animal on each lantern below.

1999

2002

2015

The year of ⎯ your birth

Gong Hei Fard Choy to you too!

In China, dragons aren't seen as scary. They're a sign of strength and good luck.

Tropic of Cancer

Hzakabo Razi ▲

MYANMAR (BURMA)

BAY OF BENGAL

Naypyitaw ●
Mount Popa
Rangoon ●

Irrawaddy River

Hanoi ●

LAOS

Vientiane ●

THAILAND

The Golden Buddha

Bangkok ●

Mekong River

Angkor Wat Temple

CAMBODIA

Phnom Penh ●

GULF OF THAILAND

Ho Chi Minh City ●

VIETNAM

GULF OF TONKIN

SOUTH CHINA SEA

Luzon

Manila ●

The Philippines is made up of more than 7,000 islands!

Palawan

SULU SEA

STRAIT OF MALACCA

Petronas Towers

Kuala Lumpur ●

Sumatra ●

● SINGAPORE

MALAYSIA

BRUNEI
Bandar Seri Begawan

Mount Kinabalu ▲

CELEBES SEA

The Petronas Towers in Malaysia are twin skyscrapers—each with 88 stories!

Sumatran Tiger

Borneo

Orangutan

MAKASSAR STRAIT

Sulawesi

Jakarta ●

JAVA SEA

INDONESIA

Java

Sunda Islands

Mount Semeru ▲

Bali

Sumbawa

Flores

Tim

INDIAN OCEAN

Sumba

100

Southeast Asia

You'll need your sea legs to explore the many thousands of islands that make up Southeast Asia. This fascinating part of the world has a tropical climate because it is close to the Equator. This means it is warm and wet all year round.

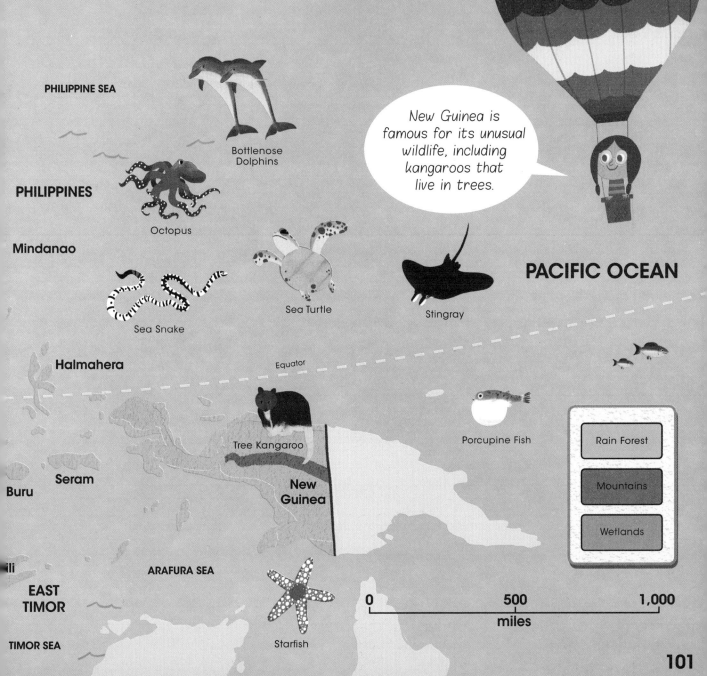

PHILIPPINE SEA

Bottlenose Dolphins

New Guinea is famous for its unusual wildlife, including kangaroos that live in trees.

PHILIPPINES

Octopus

Mindanao

PACIFIC OCEAN

Sea Snake

Sea Turtle

Stingray

Halmahera

Equator

Tree Kangaroo

Porcupine Fish

Seram

New Guinea

Buru

Rain Forest

Mountains

Wetlands

li

ARAFURA SEA

EAST TIMOR

0   500   1,000
miles

TIMOR SEA

Starfish

Swing with gibbons

The best place to see gibbons is high up in the canopy of the rain forests of Laos. Here you can stay in treehouses that are joined together with zip wires. Just like the gibbons, you won't need to touch the ground!

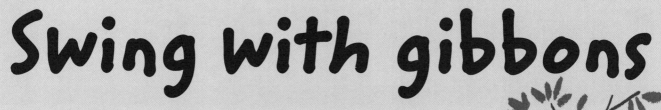

Gibbons are small apes that live in family groups. Each family has its own patch of forest.

A gibbon's arms and legs are twice as long as its body. It swings quickly through the trees, gripping on tightly with its strong hands and feet.

Gibbons love eating fruit, especially juicy figs, which they pluck fresh from the trees. They also eat leaves, flowers, seeds, shoots, and birds' eggs.

People can't swing through the trees like gibbons can, but zip wires give us an idea what it would be like!

A safety harness keeps you safely attached to the wire as you zip along!

Woohoo!

Use the grid as a guide to draw your own gibbon.

Go island hopping

Welcome to Indonesia! This extraordinary country has volcanoes, amazing wildlife, beautiful beaches, and lots more to explore. So jump on board a ferry for an island-hopping tour.

The biggest island in Indonesia is Sumatra, famous for the rare and majestic Sumatran tiger.

Surfing

Kite Surfing

Snorkeling

Singapore

Borneo

Wild animals thrive in the rain forests of Sumatra and Borneo.

Sumatra

Sumatran Tiger

Orangutan

Belitung Island

INDONESIA

Shadow Puppet Show

Danau Volcano

Java

In Java, puppets are made from leather and fixed to wooden sticks. The audience watches as shadows are cast onto a cotton screen.

Bali

Each of these travelers took a ferry journey along one of the colored routes on the map. Look for clues and match a color to each traveler.

A. I got very wet and had to paddle fast.

Color: _____

B. I had to look closely in the trees for parrots.

Color: _____

C. Shadows told a story on my adventure.

Color: _____

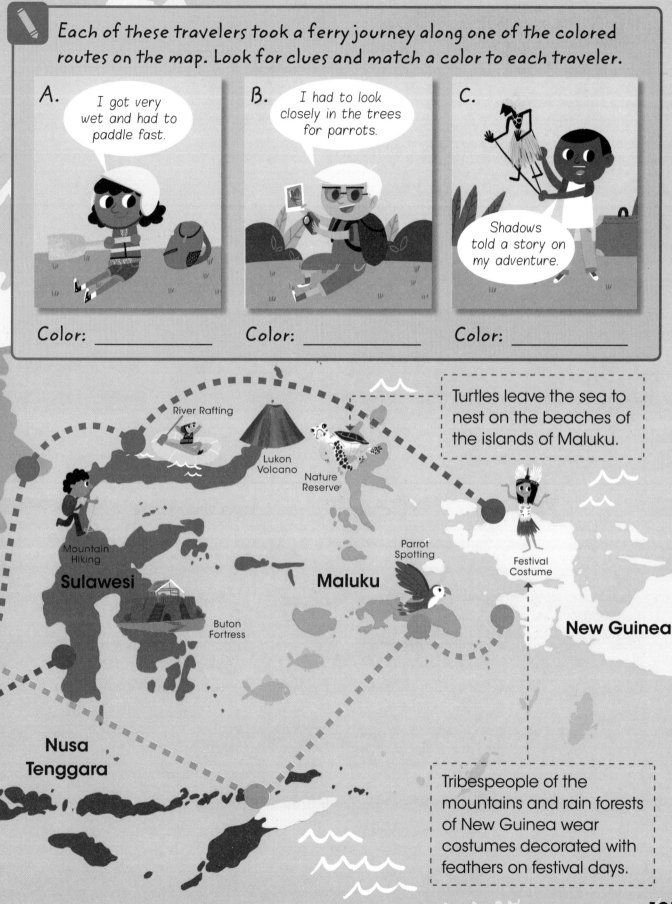

Turtles leave the sea to nest on the beaches of the islands of Maluku.

River Rafting

Lukon Volcano

Nature Reserve

Mountain Hiking

Sulawesi

Buton Fortress

Maluku

Parrot Spotting

Festival Costume

New Guinea

Nusa Tenggara

Tribespeople of the mountains and rain forests of New Guinea wear costumes decorated with feathers on festival days.

Visit a temple

You've arrived at the Grand Palace in the heart of Bangkok, the capital city of Thailand. This is a special place for Buddhists, who come to worship at the Temple of the Emerald Buddha.

The Grand Palace is a complex of buildings and statues built for the ruler of Thailand. Today it is open to the public.

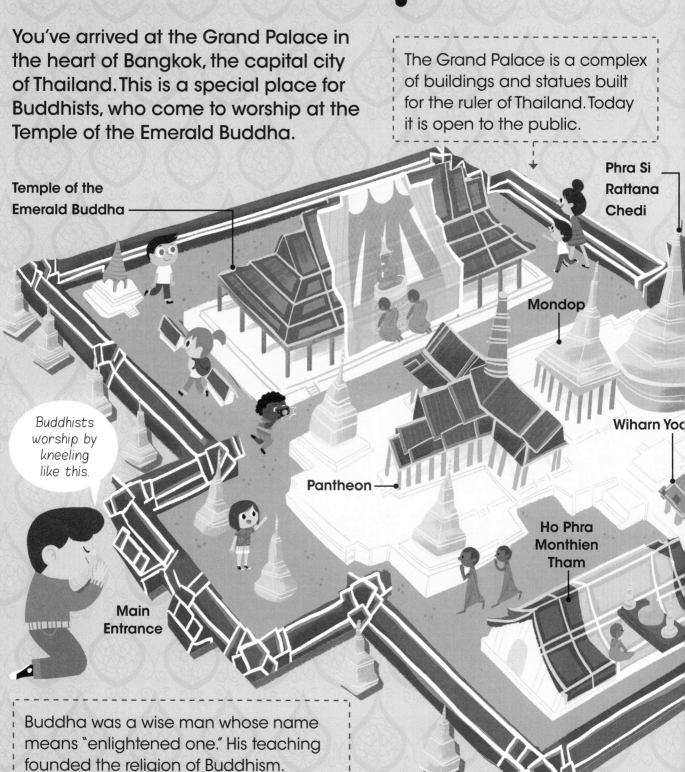

Phra Si Rattana Chedi

Temple of the Emerald Buddha

Mondop

Buddhists worship by kneeling like this.

Wiharn Yod

Pantheon

Ho Phra Monthien Tham

Main Entrance

Buddha was a wise man whose name means "enlightened one." His teaching founded the religion of Buddhism.

The Emerald Buddha is carved from a single piece of precious stone. He sits with his legs crossed in a traditional Buddhist pose of meditation.

Meditation is a way of thinking deeply to calm and relax your mind.

Follow the steps below to have a go at meditating.

1 Sit tall
Sit on the floor cross-legged, with your back, neck, and head in a straight line.

2 Relax your eyes
Let your eyes glaze over as you look into the distance.

3 Breathe deeply
Breathe steadily in through your nose, then out through your mouth. Close your eyes.

4 Focus
Focus on your breath going in and out of your body. Continue to breathe deeply and steadily.

5 Calm your mind
If you think of something else, focus again on your breathing. Meditate for about five minutes.

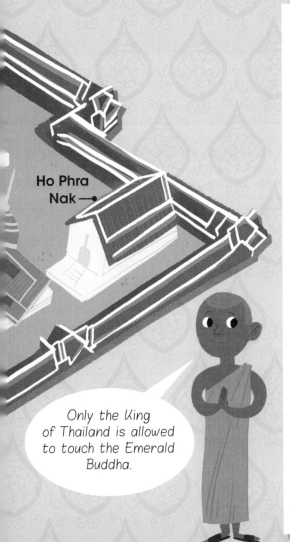

Ho Phra Nak →

Only the King of Thailand is allowed to touch the Emerald Buddha.

Australasia

Welcome to Australasia! It's a continent of great contrast, from the enormous wilderness of Australia's desert outback to the far-flung islands of the Pacific Ocean.

Bird-of-Paradise

PAPUA NEW GUINEA ▲ Mount Wilhem

Port Moresby ●

ARAFURA SEA

TORRES STRAIT

C A P E A R N H E M

GREAT BARRI

TIMOR SEA

GULF OF CARPENTARIA

INDIAN OCEAN

G R E A T S A N D Y D E S E R T

AUSTRALIA

Didgeridoo

Koala

> Uluru is a giant sandstone rock and an important place for the native Australian Aboriginal people.

●Alice Springs

Uluru

Sheep

N O R T H W E S T C A P E

G R E A T V I C T O R I A D E S E R T

Lake Eyre

Kangaroo

N U L L A R B O R   P L A I N

Darling River

● Perth

GREAT AUSTRALIAN BIGHT

Adelaide ●

Murray River

Melbourne ●

Mountains	Grasslands
Desert	Rain Forest

C A P E L E E U W I N

Great White Shark

Tasmania

Hob

S O U
E A S
C A P

Tasmanian Devil

SOUTHERN OCEAN

0   500   1,000
miles

Tiger Shark

Equator

KIRIBATI

SOLOMON SEA

SOLOMON ISLANDS

Honiara

Puffer Fish

TUVALU

Funafuti

Tokelau Islands

CORAL SEA

PACIFIC OCEAN

Octopus

VANUATU

Wallis and Futuna

SAMOA

Apia

American Samoa

Scuba Diver

New Caledonia

Port Vila

FIJI

Suva

TONGA

Niue

Speedboat

Tropic of Capricorn

Nukualofa

Brisbane

Sydney Opera House

The spectacular Sydney Opera House is designed to look like the sails of a great ship.

On special occasions, the Maoris of New Zealand perform a traditional war dance, called the haka.

Sydney

anberra

Mount Kosciuszko

Auckland

North Island

Maori Dancer

TASMAN SEA

COOK STRAIT

Wellington

South Island

NEW ZEALAND

Chatham Islands

Humpback Whale

Discover Dreamtime

Meet the indigenous Aborigine people of Australia. Their ancestors have lived here for thousands of years. Aborigine culture is based on the idea of Dreamtime—the belief in the natural spirit of animals, plants, and the land.

Images of nature are very important to the Aborigines. Pictures made up of small dots of color are painted on rocks, wood, or cloth.

There are many Aboriginal Dreamtime stories about animals. *The Tale of the Gecko* describes how a large lizard with three different patterns split into three smaller lizards.

There are more than 400 different types of Aboriginal peoples, each with their own language and cultural traditions.

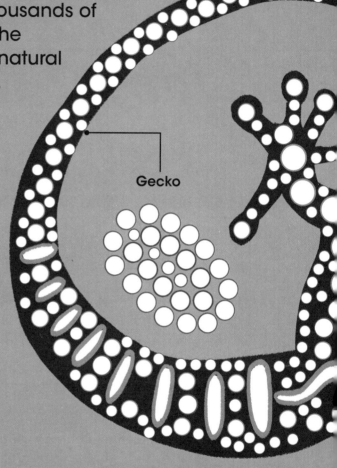

Gecko

Snorkel on the reef

Slip a snorkel on and discover the amazing underwater world of the Great Barrier Reef. The world's biggest coral reef can even be seen from space and is teeming with life!

Damselfish

Red Bass

Box Jellyfish

Box jellyfish are poisonous, so avoid their long tentacles!

Bottlenose Dolphin

Striped Surgeonfish

Coral is built by tiny animals, called polyps. Millions of them live together and build hard cases around their soft bodies. These cases join together and make up the reef.

Stingray

Coral can be lots of different shapes and colors—that's why it's so beautiful!

Giant clams are animals called mollusks that live on the reef. They have the biggest shells in the world.

Cone Shell

Giant Clam

Staghorn Coral

See exotic birds

You've explored the island of New Guinea and photographed some of its famous birds-of-paradise. Let's check out a gallery of your best snaps of these exotic wonders of nature.

Birds-of-paradise are known for their impressive feathers and displays. To attract a mate, they often perform magnificent dances to show off their colors and markings.

▶ Wilson's Bird-of-Paradise

Wilson's Bird-of-Paradise is the most colorful of them all, with two curved tail feathers.

▶ Magnificent Riflebird

Normally it's the male bird-of-paradise that has exotic feathers. The female is usually quite plain.

▶ Raggiana Bird-of-Paradise

The Magnificent Riflebird fans out its shimmering black wings, while whipping its neck to and fro.

The Raggiana Bird-of-Paradise shakes its feathers, claps its wings, and shakes its head—often while upside-down.

Greater Bird-of-Paradise

The Greater Bird-of-Paradise ruffles its feathers and flaps its wings. Then it lowers its head and turns its back to reveal brilliant yellow feathers.

King Bird-of-Paradise

What a beauty! The King Bird-of-Paradise is known for his bright blue feet.

Create your own colorful bird-of-paradise.

Look! The most spectacular of them all!

Please do not touch the photographs

Antarctica

At the bottom of the world is Antarctica. It's even colder here than the Arctic and a huge layer of ice and snow blankets the land. In winter the stormy Southern Ocean around Antarctica freezes, making Antarctica double in size.

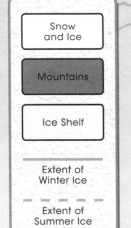

Huge chunks of ice break off the ice shelves and float out to sea as icebergs.

Weddell Seal

South Orkney Islands

WEDDELL SEA

Iceberg

Antarctic Peninsula

L A R S E N
I C E
S H E L F

Palmer Land

R O N N
I C E
S H E L

Ellsworth Land

Mount Vins

WEST ANTARCTIC

Marie B
Land

AMUNDSEN SEA

Leopard Seal

Killer Whale

King Crab

Elephant Seal

PACIFIC OCEAN

| Snow and Ice |
| Mountains |
| Ice Shelf |
| —— Extent of Winter Ice |
| ---- Extent of Summer Ice |

Giant Squid

Antarctic Cruise Ship

0   500   1,000
miles

SOUTHERN OCEAN

SOUTHERN OCEAN

Antarctic Circle

Emperor Penguin

Adélie Penguin

Queen Maud Land

Enderby Land

SOUTH AFRICA

South Africa is about 2,400 miles this way!

Halley VI Research Station

Kemp Land

A M E R Y   I C E   S H E L F

FILCHNER ICE SHELF

Dog Sled

P O L A R   P L A T E A U

Princess Elizabeth Land

DAVIS SEA

Kaiser Wilhelm II Land

S O U T H   P O L E

Queen Mary Land

Arctic Tern

Lake Vostok is buried thousands of feet beneath the ice.

T R A N S A N T A R C T I C   M O U N T A I N S

Lake Vostok

R O S S   I C E   S H E L F

EAST ANTARCTICA

Wilkes Land

McMurdo Research Station

Snow Tractor

ROSS SEA

Victoria Land

Ice Breaker

Humpback Whale

Be a scientist

It's too cold to live in Antarctica all the time, but many scientists spend the summer there. They live in research stations and collect scientific information. You can spend a day with them and help with their research.

Research stations even provide physical activities such as climbing walls!

Antarctica is an important place for the study of meteorites from space, which are preserved in the freezing conditions.

Inside the station it's snug and warm, but outside the temperature is around -60°F.

Scientists study rock, millions of years old, dug from deep beneath the surface. From this they can find out how the world's climate has changed over time.

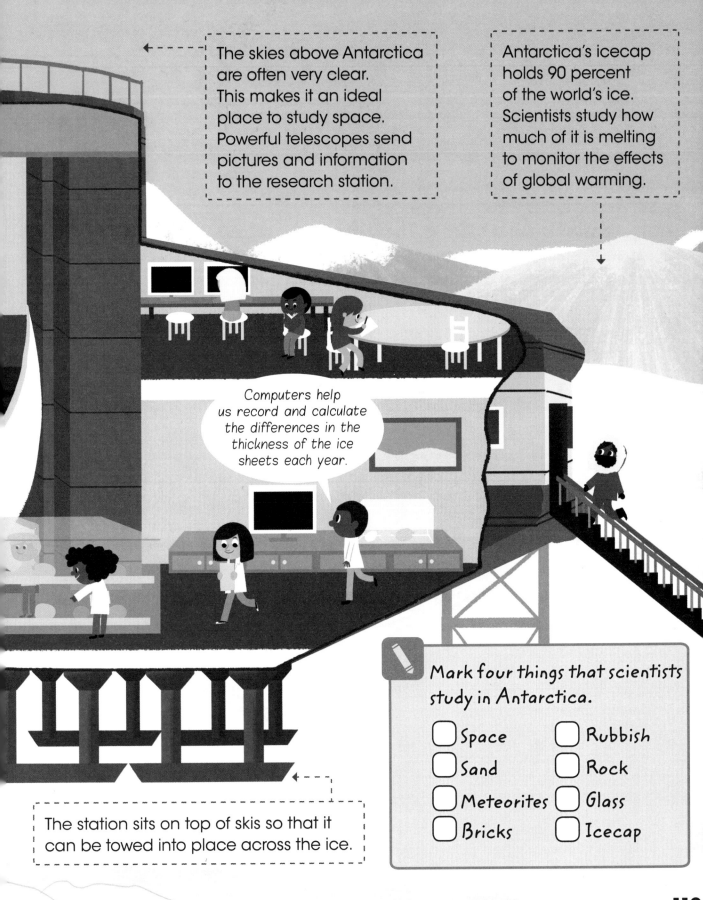

The skies above Antarctica are often very clear. This makes it an ideal place to study space. Powerful telescopes send pictures and information to the research station.

Antarctica's icecap holds 90 percent of the world's ice. Scientists study how much of it is melting to monitor the effects of global warming.

Computers help us record and calculate the differences in the thickness of the ice sheets each year.

Mark four things that scientists study in Antarctica.

☐ Space   ☐ Rubbish
☐ Sand   ☐ Rock
☐ Meteorites ☐ Glass
☐ Bricks   ☐ Icecap

The station sits on top of skis so that it can be towed into place across the ice.

Race to the South Pole

More than 100 years ago, explorers Roald Amundsen and Robert Falcon Scott and their brave teams each set off on a dangerous race. The goal was to be the first humans to reach the South Pole. Read their stories to find out who won!

ANTARCTICA

For weeks, Amundsen and Scott battled through blizzards and crossed deadly glaciers.

ROALD AMUNDSEN

On his expedition he took with him:

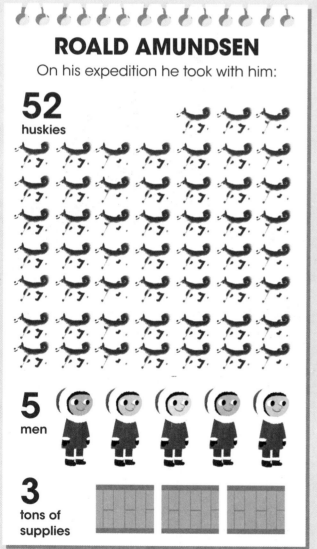

52 huskies

5 men

3 tons of supplies

ROBERT FALCON SCOTT

On his expedition he took with him:

17 men

1 ton of supplies

120

STORY MIX-UP

Number the boxes from 1 to 5 to put the story in the correct order.

November 17, 1911
Amundsen's team stopped at the edge of the Transantarctic Mountains. They had to find a route up an incredibly steep glacier.

December 14, 1911
Amundsen's team reached the South Pole. They became the first people to reach this southernmost point on Earth.

November 1, 1911
Scott set off with his full team. Later, he'd pick just a few men to do the last part of the journey, pulling their own supplies on sleds.

October 19, 1911
Amundsen set off with five men and 52 huskies to pull their sleds. The weather was heavy with fog as they crossed a number of ice crevasses.

South Pole

January 17, 1912
Scott's team reached the South Pole. They found that Amundsen had reached it five weeks earlier and with a shorter travel time.

Amundsen's route ——  —— Scott's route

Ross Ice Shelf

Amundsen's starting point

Scott's starting point

Ross Sea

Watch the penguins

The Southern Ocean around Antarctica is icy, bitterly cold, and home to many of the world's penguins. These birds are famous for their funny waddle on land, but they are superb swimmers and well adapted to the freezing weather.

Emperor penguins can dive deeper than any other bird. They stay underwater for up to 27 minutes, hunting for food.

EMPEROR PENGUIN

Penguins can't fly, but they use their wings as flippers to push themselves through the water.

Penguins have special features to help them survive. They have thick windproof and waterproof feathers, and a layer of fat next to their skin to keep them warm.

Emperor penguins are the tallest of all the penguins.

The male Emperor penguin looks after the egg, cradling it with his feet until the penguin chick hatches.

EMPEROR PENGUIN

Height	45 inches
Weight	65 pounds
Swimming speed	7 mph

ADELIE PENGUIN

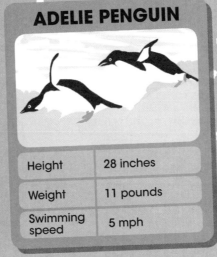

Height	28 inches
Weight	11 pounds
Swimming speed	5 mph

GENTOO PENGUIN

Height	28 inches
Weight	12 pounds
Swimming speed	23 mph

 Pick your penguins and play the feature-comparing game!

HOW TO PLAY

You will need: ● A pen ● Paper ● A die

1 Two players choose a set of penguins each from above and below.

2 Take turns to roll the die. On each roll, follow the key below to see which set of penguins wins the category.

3 Keep score after each roll of the die and add up the totals after 12 rounds. The player with the highest score wins!

● Tallest   ⚁ Shortest   ⚂ Fastest   ⚃ Slowest   ⚄ Heaviest   ⚅ Lightest

CHINSTRAP PENGUIN

Height	27 inches
Weight	9 pounds
Swimming speed	20 mph

MACARONI PENGUIN

Height	27 inches
Weight	10 pounds
Swimming speed	9 mph

KING PENGUIN

Height	37 inches
Weight	33 pounds
Swimming speed	4.8 mph

Famous Landmarks

Our world is filled with so many incredible landmarks. Some are natural wonders, such as towering volcanoes and dramatic canyons. Others, like mighty statues and ornate temples, show what humans can create.

The White House, United States The official home and workplace of the President of the United States.

Ericsson Globe, Sweden The largest hemispherical building in the world, meaning it's shaped like a giant ball cut in half.

Mount Rushmore, United States Massive 60-foot-high sculpture carved into Mount Rushmore of four previous presidents of the United States.

Brandenburg Gate, Germany A three-hundred-year-old arch in Berlin, built as a monument to peace.

Grand Canyon, United States A steep-sided canyon carved by the Colorado River, and 277 miles long.

Angel of the North, United Kingdom Created by artist Antony Gormley in 1998, with a wingspan as big as a jumbo jet.

Chichén Itza, Mexico Ruins of an ancient Mayan city with pyramids, temples, and other stone structures.

Colosseum, Italy An oval amphitheater in the center of Rome, built by the ancient Romans. It was used for gladiatorial battles.

APEX Telescope, Chile A massive radio telescope 16,732 feet above sea level that picks up sounds from space.

Parthenon, Greece Ruins of an ancient Greek temple in Athens, dedicated to the goddess Athena.

Christ the Redeemer, Brazil Giant statue perched high on a hill, overlooking the city of Rio de Janeiro.

Bran Castle, Romania Historic royal palace said to be the home of the fictional character Count Dracula.

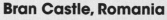

Hassan Tower, Morocco A minaret (Islamic tower) built nearly a thousand years ago.

Great Mosque of Djenné, Mali The largest mud-brick building in the world.

Table Mountain, South Africa
A flat-topped mountain overlooking the city of Cape Town.

Winter Palace, Russia The official home of the Russian royal family from 1732 to 1917, now a museum.

The Motherland Calls, Russia A gigantic statue, 279 feet tall, commemorating the Battle of Stalingrad.

Mehrangarh Fort, India A massive fort, built from red sandstone on
a cliff over five hundred years ago.

Attar's Tomb, Iran An octagonal tomb with onion-shaped dome, covered in green, yellow, and blue tiles.

Dome of the Rock, Jerusalem An Islamic shrine on Temple Mount— the first domed mosque ever to be built.

Three Gorges Dam, China A hydroelectric dam that spans the Yangtze River and is the world's largest power station.

Torii Gate, Japan A traditional Japanese gate, nearly 900 years old, said to be where the spiritual and human worlds meet.

Mount Fuji, Japan An active volcano and the country's tallest peak at 12,388 feet.

Angkor Wat Temple, Cambodia The largest religious monument in the world. Its name means City of Temples.

The Golden Buddha, Thailand A solid gold statue of Buddha, housed in Wat Traimit temple.

Uluru, Australia A massive sandstone rock, sacred to the Australian Aboriginal people—about 700 million years old.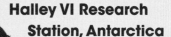

Halley VI Research Station, Antarctica A scientific research base resting on giant skis.

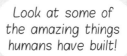

Look at some of the amazing things humans have built!

Index

Answers

Page 11

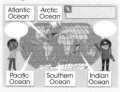

Pages 14-15
Metropolitan Museum of Art–3,
One World Trade Center–2,
Brooklyn Children's Museum–1,
Times Square–2, Central Park–1
Grand Central Station–3

Page 18

Page 22
A–36 in, B–38 in,
C–32 in, D–34 in

Pages 24-25
Correct numbers, left to
right: 2, 1, 4, 5, 3

Page 31
F6–Sayacmarca, D4–Intipata,
B5–Inti Punku, A3–Machu Picchu

Pages 32-33

Pages 34-35

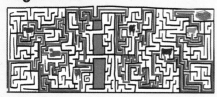

Pages 38-39

Pages 42-43

Page 47

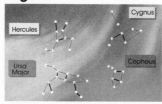

Pages 48-49
Eiffel Tower–8, Notre Dame–4, Arc
de Triomphe–2, Sacré-Cœur–3,
Musée du Louvre–2, Panthéon–7

Pages 50-51
The Gherkin–E, Big Ben–C,
The Shard–D, St. Paul's
Cathedral–B, Tower Bridge–A

Pages 56-57

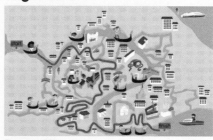

Page 65
Who was the king?
Answer: Pharaoh Khufu

Pages 66-67

Pages 70-71
Elephants–9, Buffalo–16, Lions–5,
Rhinoceroses–8, Pronghorns–7,
Zebra–5, Giraffes–9, Leopards–2

Page 79
Emblem B

Page 81
5,758 miles

Page 83

Pages 88-89

Pages 94-95
A–false, B–true, C–false, D–true

Page 99
2002–Horse, 2015–Sheep

Pages 104-105
A–red, B–pink, C–blue

Pages 112-113

Page 119
Space, meteorites, rock, icecap

Page 121
1–October 19, 1911
2–November 1, 1911
3–November 17, 1911
4–December 14, 1911
5–January 17, 1912